DISCOVERING DANIEL BLUE

MY SEARCH FOR SIGNIFICANCE, PURPOSE, AND LEGACY

LES ROBINSON

KP PUBLISHING COMPANY

ISBN: 978-1-960001-75-7 Hardcover
ISBN: 978-1-960001-76-4 Paperback)
ISBN: 978-1-960001-77-1 (eBook)

Library of Congress Control Number: Pending

Editor: Laurel J. Davis, Empathy Editorial
Cover Design: Juan Roberts, Creative Lunacy
Literary Director: Sandra Slayton James

Published by:

KP Publishing Company
Publisher of Fiction, Nonfiction & Children's Books
Las Vegas, NV 89117
www.kp-pub.com

Printed in the United States of America

DEDICATION

I dedicate this book to the loving memory of my
beautiful mother, Janet Laverne Shankle, a woman equipped
with a Bible and a switch, who loved, fed, shaped, and prepared
me for life's challenges. She prayed for me, introduced me to
my Lord and Savior, Jesus Christ, and told me that I could do
and be anything I wanted to do or be in life.

Janet Robinson
(Les Robinson's Mother)'
January 4, 1934 to October 13, 2022

THE WOMAN WITH THE BIBLE AND A SWITCH

Recently I celebrated my 66th time around the sun, and I arrived here by overcoming and enduring many hardships, challenges, and mistakes, all because of a little tough woman who had a Bible and a switch.

I was somehow able to stay out of trouble. Instead, I became an athlete, a Boy Scout, an honor student, a musician, an actor, a writer, and a pastor—all because of a little persistent woman with a Bible and a switch.

I was blessed to be a husband, a father, an uncle, a mentor, a coach, and a friend because of the loving atmosphere she raised us in, because of this little strong-willed woman, and all that she did, with the Bible and that switch.

The Bible was her constitution, her map, and her guide. Her switch was her enforcer of life-saving values, and she made us abide.

The results of what she instilled (the Bible) and how she upheld it (the switch) have left me with countless, priceless deposits of wisdom, knowledge, insight, and foresight.

She protected, fed, taught, and loved us, but her greatest gift was that she introduced us to a love greater than her own, that being the Lord Jesus Christ, my Savior, the greatest Friend I have ever known.

Because of all this, I will always love, honor, and miss my sweet little mother, who loved me with all she had: the Bible and a Switch.

—Les Robinson

CONTENTS

Dedication   *v*

The Woman with the Bible and a Switch   *vii*

Preface   *xi*

Introduction   *xiii*

Chapter 1   The Discovery   1

Chapter 2   Daniel Blue's Legacy   23

Chapter 3   My Beginning   29

Chapter 4   I Got a "C"   33

Chapter 5   From Land Park to Oak Park   39

Chapter 6   1969   55

Chapter 7   High School Daze   61

Chapter 8   Panthers and Gators   75

Photos   The Legacy of Daniel Blue   93

Chapter 9   "Hell No!"   109

Chapter 10   After SFSU   117

Chapter 11   Show Biz?   131

Chapter 12   The Kingdom   145

Chapter 13   Living the Legacy   161

Acknowledgments   *165*

About the Author   *167*

Milestones in the Life and Legacy of Daniel Blue   *169*

Bibliography   *177*

PREFACE

"We all, at some point in life, conduct a personal inner search for significance, purpose, and legacy."

—Les Robinson

In Les Robinson's personal story, *Discovering Daniel Blue: My Search for Significance, Purpose, and Legacy,* you'll read about some of his experiences and many of the lessons he learned growing up in an American ghetto as a young, fatherless black man in the turbulent Sixties and Seventies.

You'll see his manifold levels of disappointment and frustration, along with some of his triumphs, as he recalls his search for answers to some of life's most intriguing questions, like *Who am I? Why am I here?* and *What is my ultimate purpose in life?*

You'll travel with him through his maze-like journey as he navigates periods of confusion and hopelessness until, at the seemingly lowest point of his life, he makes a chance discovery of an ancestor, Daniel Blue, a former slave and pioneer who struck it rich mining for gold and brought an end to slavery in California.

The revelation of Daniel Blue's largely unsung contributions to the world brings Les face to face with God, himself, and a new state of awareness about his own significance, purpose, and legacy. In particular, the parallels of Les' and Daniel's lives reveal that the sovereign God of the universe has led and shaped them both to bring about love and harmony with God and man through the work of racial reconciliation and solidarity towards the continued healing of our nation and world.

> *"We must learn to live together as brothers, or perish together as fools."*
>
> —Dr. Martin Luther King, Jr.

INTRODUCTION

Have you ever wondered what happens when a race or people have no knowledge or understanding of their traditions, history, and culture? How do you think they would act if they had no sense of significance, purpose, or legacy? How do you think they would act if, for hundreds of years, they were conditioned to think they were nothing, they could be nothing, they could have nothing, they could do nothing, and they were less than nothing?

That was the plight of many African Americans in the United States during the 20th Century. I know this because I saw it, I heard it, and I lived it. It seemed as if we were allowed to go only so far, climb only so high, and achieve only so much because of systematic racism.

But for some reason, I never allowed the limitations of racism to affect or govern my thoughts, dreams, or expectations. I have always had a desire to explore and venture out into places and spaces that were not necessarily "black." I wanted to try different things, like scuba diving, golf, tennis, race car driving, and flying planes.

I remember an experience in elementary school. My teacher asked us what we all wanted to be when we grew up. When it was my turn, I said I wanted to be a lawyer because I enjoyed watching "Perry Mason," a lawyer on TV. I was very impressed by how he gathered evidence that enabled him to solve a myriad of difficult criminal cases. My teacher told me instead that I should consider pursuing other professions, such as a janitor or warehouseman. This, in spite of the fact that I had a reading and comprehension level two grades higher than anyone else in the class.

And then I remember Rodney King. On March 3, 1991, CHP officers pulled King over for speeding on a Los Angeles freeway. An African American, King was on probation for a robbery conviction. Four officers arrested and cuffed him, threw him to the ground, and began to beat him mercilessly with their billy clubs, not knowing that they were being videotaped by a citizen named George Holliday. Mr. Holliday's recording found its way to every local and major news outlet that broadcast the beating over and over again. The CHP officers were subsequently charged and indicted, the Rodney King trial began, closing arguments were delivered, and the whole nation anxiously awaited the jury's decision.

On April 29,1992, after seven days of deliberation, the jury acquitted all four officers of assault and three of them for use of excessive force. Because of these acquittals, riots broke out in Los Angeles. In five days of rioting, burning, and looting, sixty people were killed, 2,300 more were injured, and 1,100 buildings were damaged or destroyed at a cost totaling more than one billion dollars in property damage.

I can recall a particular discussion about the trial at work. At the time, I was a courier for FedEx. We were working the morning sort when a white co-worker approached me.

"Les, what is up with your people?", he began. "Why are they so angry? Why are they burning down LA? Why do they care so much about Rodney King? He was a crook!"

I said, "Bro, these riots have nothing to do with Rodney King. Those people don't even care about Rodney King. They are rioting and burning things down because they are sick and tired of 200-plus years of bigotry, lies, double standards, and injustice."

The whole world saw the recorded video evidence of four white officers beating a harmless black man as if he were a dangerous animal even though his hands were cuffed, and he was not violent or a threat. The beating of Rodney King was clearly unnecessary and thus was, without question, a demonstration of excessive, abusive force. So, when a jury acquitted the CHP officers whom the public saw as guilty, that limiting ceiling had appeared once again, only this time in the arena of justice. As a result, we witnessed in five days of rioting many years of suppressed anger. In those five days of destruction and disturbance, we saw 200-plus years of frustration and disappointment.

How can we end this? How do we heal? How do we change this narrative and abandon these senseless cycles of hatred, fear, and injustice?

I've often wondered, if African Americans knew who we really are and where we came from, if we knew about our African traditions, culture, and contributions, would we be the same? If we knew about the many significant contributions we've made in the world, would that foster in us a greater sense of dignity, pride, and self-respect?

For that matter, I wonder if the world knew who we really are and where we came from, if they knew about our traditions, culture, and contributions, would they view us the same way? If the world considered the many significant contributions that we of African descent have made in the world, would that foster in them a greater respect for us?

Thinking about it further, if African Americans knew about the legacies of our respective ancestors, would we be different? If we knew we were of royal blood, descendants of great kings and queens among history's wealthiest kingdoms and of inventors and pioneers among history's greatest scientists and explorers, would we approach life and its challenges differently? And if the world were aware, would they view us differently?

Yes, I believe we all would be different and have different perspectives if we all had fuller knowledge of African and African American history. I feel this way because I changed after I discovered that I was a descendant in the legacy of Daniel Blue. After I found out who he was, what he did, how he lived, what he lived for, and who he lived for, I indeed changed.

This knowledge has empowered and encouraged me to live a more purposeful and courageous life. It has inspired me to intentionally live a life of legacy and faith that my children and grandchildren and their children will value and want to emulate.

I hope that, after reading this book, you too will discover your Daniel Blue and the earthly legacy that's been left for you. More importantly, I hope that you will discover *you,* the person God has intentionally called to Earth to live a life of significance, purpose, and legacy in Him.

CHAPTER 1

MY DISCOVERY

The world in 2018 was a weird one, full of surprises, turmoil, and change. President Donald Trump had been in office one year. The median cost of gas nationally was $2.72 a gallon (Statista.com), and the median cost to own a new home in the United States was about $326,400 (FREDSTLOUISFED.org). The number one hit on the pop music charts was "God's Plan" by Drake (EN.WIKIPEDIA.ORG). In February, a gunman opened fire at Marjory Stoneman Douglas High School in Parkland, Florida, killing seventeen students and staff members. The Winter Olympics Games were held in Pyeongchang, South Korea. On May 19th, in front of an estimated 1.9 billion television viewers, African American actress Meghan Markle married Prince Harry of Great Britain and became the Duchess of Sussex. California became the sixth state to legalize the sale of recreational marijuana. Physician Larry Nassar was sentenced to up to 175 years in prison for sexually abusing more than 250 girls. And France, in front of 3.4 billion television viewers, won the FIFA World Cup in soccer four to two over Croatia.

Yep, 2018 turned out to be a real doozy!

It was a very challenging year for me as well personally because, after twenty-one years of marriage, my second wife decided she wanted a divorce. This revelation caused me a great deal of sadness, confusion, and despair. I never imagined I'd be dealing with a divorce in my sixties. I was nearing retirement and was starting to think about all the things that come along with it. Now, instead of thinking about that, I was thinking about the challenges of divorce and the uncertainty of what tomorrow might bring.

After being married for twenty-one years, how would I navigate the prospect of being alone? How badly would this affect my family and friends? How much change would occur in my life? Would I be able to survive financially? I was fighting hard to be positive in this negative situation, but it was a hard fight because now I was alone and living in the large five-bedroom house that God had miraculously given us sixteen years earlier. I felt like a total failure because this was not the kind of legacy I wanted to leave to my children and grandchildren. How could God get any glory out of my life in this condition?

Not long after this, in late 2019, three students were killed in a mass shooting at Saugus High School in Santa Clarita, California, where I had established the first Fellowship of Christian Athletes Huddle. A few months later, COVID-19 erupted worldwide; and a short time after that, I was diagnosed with cancer and was dismissed from a job that I really loved.

Going through a divorce, along with the challenges of having cancer and lacking employment, soon exhausted my resources, and the bills and calls from creditors soon began to pile up. To make things worse, my mother's health was starting to decline due to sugar diabetes and kidney failure. She was now in her seventeenth year of kidney dialysis treatments and maintaining a comfortable lifestyle was becoming very difficult for her. It was not hard to see she was beginning to fade away.

During this time, I felt so alone and isolated. I felt as though everything and everybody I loved had either abandoned me or was being taken away from me. I thought I had experienced some tough times in life before but, because of what was happening now, I was at an all-time low.

On the outside, 1 put up a front and just went through the motions of living. But on the inside, I was a dead man walking. I felt as though no one really cared about me or my situation. All hell had broken loose in my life, and I felt there was nothing I could do about it. I had nowhere to go for comfort or relief. I had no one to turn to who could help me . . . but God. So, in my deepest despair, I cried out to Him to straighten out my life. It seemed like I was a character in the movie "Groundhog Day," repeating the same scene day after day and night after night.

Only God knows how many nights my pillows were soaking wet because I had cried or prayed myself to sleep, only to wake up the next day and do it all over again. I asked God in prayer over and over, *What is this all about? Did I do something wrong? Is this a punishment, a correction, or a growth opportunity?* I asked Him time and time again, *Am I Job? Am I Job?* I would say to him, *I know how You delivered and restored Job. Do You have the same plan for me?*

All I could do was to hang on to the promises in God's Word, pray, and trust Him to bring me through. It seemed as though I would be in this state of fog and uncertainty forever. But somehow, some way, I'm sure by God's grace, I was able to hang on to His Word. Some of the Scriptures that sustained me during these difficult times included:

> *"The temptations in your life are not different from what others experience. And God is faithful. He will not allow the temptation to be more than you can stand. When you are tempted, he will show you a way out so that you can endure."*
>
> —1 Corinthians 10:13 (NLT)

> *"Yes, and everyone who wants to live a godly life in Christ Jesus will suffer persecution."*
>
> —2 Timothy 3:12 (NLT)

> *"I will bless the Lord at all times: his praise shall continually be in my mouth. My soul shall make her boast in the Lord: the humble shall hear thereof and be glad. O magnify the Lord with me and let us exalt his name together. I sought the Lord, and he heard me, and delivered*

me from all my fears. . . . This poor man cried, and the Lord
heard him, and saved him out of all his troubles. The angel
of the Lord encampeth round about them that fear him, and
delivereth them. O taste and see that the Lord is good:
blessed is the man that trusteth in him. O fear the Lord, ye
his saints: for there is no want to them that fear him. The
young lions do lack and suffer hunger: but they that seek
the Lord shall not want any good thing. . . . The righteous
cry, and the Lord heareth, and delivereth them out of all
their troubles. The Lord is nigh unto them that are of a
broken heart; and saveth such as be of a contrite spirit.
Many are the afflictions of the righteous: but the Lord
delivereth him out of them all. . . . The Lord redeemeth the
soul of his servants: and none of them that trust in him
shall be desolate."

—Psalms 34:1-4, 6-10, 17-19, 22 (KJV)

"But the salvation of the righteous is of the Lord:
He is their strength in the time of trouble. And the
Lord shall help them and deliver them: He shall deliver
them from the wicked, and save them, because they
trust in him."

—Psalm 37:39-40 (KJV)

And, He did! It was during this darkest, most painful time in my life that God allowed me to stumble into what I had been searching for all my life. Namely, the knowledge of my significance, purpose, and legacy.

My prayers to God for years would sound something like this:

> God, please don't let my living be in vain. Please work with me and allow me to do something that will cause positive change in this world. Allow me to serve my generation well, like Your servant King David served his. Lord, use me to Your glory and honor, and never let me bring shame to You or to my family. Oh God, I want to leave an honorable legacy to You, my children, and my grandchildren. I would like You and my descendants to be proud of the life I lived. Please help me to find those people and places meant for me. Lord, please don't let me mess things up. I want You to get all the glory out of my life. I thank You for all that You've done for me, all that You are doing for me right now, and what You're going to do for me in the future. In Jesus's name, I pray. Amen.

The significance, purpose, and legacy of my life began to literally unfold before me on Saturday, July 15, 2017, at a family barbeque hosted by my brother Don.

Don was ten months younger than me but for most of my life was taller, which made us very close but also very competitive. He was the first person beside my mother and father that I can remember from my earliest childhood. Growing up, we did almost everything together. We slept in the same bed, wore the same clothes, and swam, played football, and ran track together. We also got into a lot of mischief together and, inevitably, we got many spankings together, too.

On this particular day, Don had just finished having a total knee reconstruction surgery and I wanted to go home to Sacramento, spend some time with him, and assist with his recovery. This visit would also be an opportunity for me to take a small vacation before beginning final preparations with my football staff and team prior to the 2018 season.

It was a beautiful, hot summer day in Sacramento. Probably twenty-five guests were at Don's house that day, mostly family and friends. My brother is a great host and cook. He's very hospitable and loves to entertain. That's why I nicknamed him "Chef Boyardee." As usual, there was plenty of good food, beverages, and music. Don had created a perfect party atmosphere, with several small groups and conversations going on that made for lots of laughing, dancing, and games.

This party was going to be special because our cousin, Andree Reed Thomas, was there and we would get to learn more about my father's side of the family. Andree was the daughter of my father's younger stepbrother, Andrè Reed, who was just seven years older than me. We never had the opportunity to know this side of the family, my father's side, because my father and mother divorced when I was eleven.

As I engaged in conversation with Andree, I mentioned that I could trace my family's roots all the way back to the slave ship on my mother's Turner-Hill side but that I knew almost nothing about my father's family history.

At that point, Andree looked at me with a very peculiar smile on her face and nonchalantly said seven words that absolutely rocked my world.

"Have you ever heard of Daniel Blue?"

There was a long pause because I really thought she was joking, and then I replied, "Who is Daniel Blue?"

"Just google Daniel Blue of Sacramento," she said.

I immediately pulled my phone out of my pocket. What I discovered from my quick Google search changed everything. It changed the way I thought about myself and my place in the world. It altered the course of my life. It affected everything I thought and everything I knew, and it uncovered a whole new dimension of myself that I was not aware of. This revelation ignited within me an emotional tsunami.

My Google search yielded a number of comprehensive biographical articles about Daniel Blue..The first one I came across was from Rootsweb.com titled "Daniel Blue, An African American Pioneer." I have since found several other online sources that give rich information about Daniel Blue. These other sources include the article, "How the Founder of California's First Black Church Fought Its Last Known Slavery Case" by Asal Ehsanipour for *The California Report Magazine,* and "Rescue of a Slave Child" for the website *Gold Chains: The Hidden History of Slavery in California. Gold Chains* is a collaboration between KQED, the American Civil Liberties Union of Northern CA, the California Historical Society, Laura Atkins, and the Equal Justice Society.

I discovered that Daniel Blue was a black pioneer who arrived in Sacramento, California, on September 2, 1849, on a wagon train from Monroe County, Kentucky. He was a former slave, brought to the state during The Gold Rush by the younger brother of his slave master. While in Sacramento, Daniel married Lucinda Luny from Alabama, and between 1851 and 1861, they had five children: William, Daniel Jr., Laura, Annie, and Henrietta. William and Laura both passed away at the age of nine.

Daniel soon struck gold, literally, along the Sacramento River. He was able to buy some land, build a home, and start a laundry business around the sight of today's Amtrak train station on 4th and I Streets. His property was next to the property of Peter Burnett, California's first governor and a racist who created and pushed for exclusionary laws against blacks and other people of color in the state. This fact only helped to develop and fuel Daniel's passion for justice.

Contrary to popular belief, California was no sanctuary for African Americans and other minorities even though the state was admitted into the Union as slave free. Slavery and the attitudes that affirmed it were still alive and well beyond September 9, 1850, when California was officially admitted. Just like Daniel's slave master and his brother did, slave owners from other states were drawn to the prospects of striking gold in California, and they brought their slaves with them, thousands of them. Couple this with the state's resulting accelerated growth, combined with corresponding greed and its close companions of corruption and lawlessness, Daniel decided to put his passion into action.

In 1850, Daniel and two fellow black pioneers, brothers Barney and George Fletcher from Maryland, founded the first African American church on the West Coast, in his home. Originally named Bethel, it was later renamed St. Andrews African Methodist Episcopal (AME) Church, and it was open to white worshippers as well as people of color. Within three years, Daniel utilized the church as a refuge and central hub for social justice and anti-slavery activism in California.

He and Lucinda also started a school in their home, initially for black, Native American, and Asian American children who were being discriminated against. The state refused to allot funds to the school, so the Blues successfully relied on donations from the local community to keep the school going.

The presence of both a church and a school operating out of their home allowed the Blues a unique opportunity. Because St. Andrews welcomed white congregants, daughters Henrietta and Annie and son Daniel Jr. were allowed to attend local schools, making them the first non-white students in California to attend public schools with whites.

As ground zero for social justice in Sacramento and the state of California, St. Andrews AME Church hosted the first (November

20-22, 1855) and the second (December 9-12,1856) statewide meetings of The California State Convention of Colored Citizens (CSCCC). These first two "Colored Conventions" in the state focused on voting rights and the court testimony rights, respectively, for African American Californians. Finally, in 1863, after eight long years of tireless activism spearheaded and forged by Daniel Blue, the desired laws were passed.

The next year, in 1864, "Uncle Daniel," as he became affectionately known in Sacramento, made what some at the time called "his most indelible mark on history" in California when he fought for and secured the freedom of twelve-year-old Edith. She was an illegally detained and abused slave girl from Missouri who was now in the grips of Walter Gammon, a local farmer from Tennessee.

Thanks to Daniel's lobbying for blacks' right to testify against whites in court, he filed a writ of habeas corpus in court that forced Mr. Gammon to bring Edith before the judge. Witnesses came forth in court to testify to Mr. Gammon's foul mistreatment of Edith, including restraining her, beating her, leaving her without clothing, and neglecting her care. Mr. Gammon claimed that she was with him of her own free choice. But Daniel Blue petitioned the judge to make him her legal guardian. The judge agreed based in large part on the witnesses' testimony.

Edith's freedom has become known as the last slavery case in California. Thanks to Daniel Blue's passion, wisdom, and tenacity. It's just unfortunate that fifteen years had to pass after its admission to the Union as a presumed "free" state. Still, even the liberation of Edith probably wouldn't have come when it did because of the previous laws that prohibited certain testimony by people of color.

Daniel Blue, died in 1884 at the age of eighty-eight years old. A news article written at the time had this to say about him:

> "For a Sacramentan to have said that he did not know Uncle Daniel Blue was to argue his ignorance of the city and his people . . . and (he) went to his rest known of all his fellow citizens with fewer to speak ill of him than falls to the lot of most men."

This discovery of Daniel Blue, was crazy! I was actually reading about *my* family! These were people whose names I had never heard of, members of my family I never knew existed. I was just introduced to Daniel Blue, a Sacramento pioneer who was my great-great-great-grandfather! In those newspaper articles, the only names I did recognize were my grandmother's (Lola Reed) and my uncle's (Andrè Reed).

I didn't know how to act, what to do, what to say, or how to feel. I was in total shock. All different kinds of emotions inside of me surged deep enough to drown in. I felt proud, but I was also angry, hurt, and confused all at the same time. And I was filled with questions.

How did this happen? How could this be? How do I process this? How did I miss this information? How did it escape me? Is this some kind of sick joke? Someone please tell me how in the world, at this age, having grown up in Sacramento—how did I never, not even once hear the name of my great-great-great-grandfather, Daniel Blue? Am I dreaming?

How is it that I'd never read his name in a Sacramento or American history book? How is it that a man who lived and fought so courageously for the freedom, justice, and equal rights of everyone, be totally erased from the annals of history?

Was he not a Sacramento pioneer? Was he not a California pioneer? Did he not play a major role in state and national history? Did he not establish the first and oldest African American church on the Pacific coast?

Was he not one of the most ardent and courageous fighters against slavery and injustice in California? Did He not fight the racist efforts of Peter Burnett, the first governor of California, a known racist and proponent of slavery, who happened to be one of his neighbors?

Peter Burnett led a wagon train to the Oregon Territory in 1843 and was elected to the Oregon legislature where he authored and passed a law that excluded freed African Americans from residing in that state. The "Peter Hardeman Burnett's Lash Law" allowed whites to keep slaves for three years, after which the slaves were to be freed but were required to leave the Oregon territory or be whipped.

Daniel Blue, on the other hand, fought boldly in the courts of California to free slaves and secure equal rights not only for African Americans, but for all people.

Because of this, in 1860, at 1:00 in the morning, an arsonist set fire to the home that Daniel Blue shared with his wife and children, at 9th and F Streets. If not for his neighbor, General Reddington, who rescued, fed, and cared for them, they would have perished. In 1863, someone tried to burn down the school at Daniel Blue's church, but they rebuilt it and continued to educate minority children.

Most people would have quit, turned tail, and run, but not Daniel Blue. He courageously continued his quest to help give people an opportunity to live better lives.

A California State commemorative plaque at 7th Street between G and H Streets marks the original location of St. Andrews AME Church, the church Daniel Blue founded in 1850. Unfortunately, the plaque is placed in the most obscure location imaginable for a commemoration: on the back wall of the Sacramento County Courthouse parking lot, adjacent to the Regional Transit Public Transportation train tracks. Why would anyone place a plaque in commemoration of such great historical value in a location as obscure as this? Would a plaque to honor presidents George Washington or Abraham Lincoln have been so hidden? Why not move it to the front of the Sacramento County Courthouse for all to see?

A commemorative plaque is also placed on Daniel Blue's grave. So how is it that his name and accomplishments are not mentioned in California's history books? How is it that his name and accomplishments are not rehearsed in the history classes of our state's elementary, middle, and high schools? We heard and learned about Peter Burnett,

John Sutter, and Kit Carson. Why didn't we hear of and learn about Daniel Blue? Why isn't there a Sacramento or California school or street bearing his name? How do you hide, ignore, or disregard a man's contributions and existence who gave so much to his community and state? Daniel Blue was a man of resolve, integrity, and great faith in God. He loved and served everyone with intentionality and genuine good will.

As I sat there at Don's barbeque and read these articles about my formidable ancestor, I was so overwhelmed and surprised by this revelation that I didn't know how to act in that moment. I needed to get away. I needed to be alone. So, I slipped outside, and I wept.

After the initial shock of discovering Daniel Blue wore off, I became increasingly angry about the failure of Sacramento, the state, and the nation to recognize and include my great-great-great-grandfather in the recordings of history. I knew I had to tell his story. I wanted everyone to know his name and who he was. I wanted everyone to know of the great and admirable things that Daniel Blue did, and what it cost him to do them. I wanted everyone to know the truth about what was really going on in the state of California back in the early 1800s.

The very first thing I wanted to do was find his gravesite so that I could visit, honor him, and pray. Through research, I discovered he was buried at East Lawn Memorial Park, located at 4300 Folsom Blvd. in Sacramento. When I arrived, I informed the front office staff I had an ancestor buried in their cemetery and I wanted directions to his gravesite. The receptionist asked to be excused so that she could check the computer in the back office. After about ten minutes, she returned and said she couldn't find Daniel Blue in their system.

Fortunately, while she was in the back, I just happened to pick up and browse through a copy of their cemetery brochure entitled "East Lawn Historical Review." In a section titled "Forgotten Pioneers at East Lawn," I found Daniel Blue's name along with a short description:

> *Daniel Blue, St. Andrews African Methodist Episcopal*
> *Church was organized in his home in 1850 – the oldest*
> *African American Church on the Pacific Coast.*

I also noticed that next to the description was the number "17" in parenthesis. "Here he is right here," I said to the receptionist. "I found his name and information here on page fifteen, among the Forgotten Pioneers at East Lawn." I then asked her what the "17" meant and she explained that he was buried in East Lawn's New Helvetia section.

New Helvetia started in 1849 as a burial ground for Sutter's Fort and was at Alhambra and J Streets, which is now occupied by Sutter Middle School. In 1954, the city of Sacramento moved nearly five thousand burial plots from the New Helvetia section to East Lawn and placed them in a mass grave. Corner walls border this section, with a few gravestones marking some of the people buried there. Among them I found the gravestone for Daniel Blue, which said:

My Discovery

Daniel Blue 1811-1899
In whose house St. Andrews African Methodist Episcopal
church, the oldest African American congregation on the
Pacific Coast, was organized in 1850 and other members of
the Sacramento area African American community laid to
rest at that site.

As I exited my car and walked towards the area of his gravesite, I wondered why anyone would just exhume five thousand burial plots and bury them in a mass grave? Did anyone care or contest it? Did anyone voice their opinion or make a stink? I also questioned if this was truly where Daniel Blue's remains were.

I spent about an hour or so there at his headstone, trying to get some perspective, praying, thanking God for Daniel Blue's life, and reflecting on what He had allowed him to do. I stood there in awe; trying to take it all in and maximize this moment in time. I was thinking about this revelation for me of Daniel Blue's life and what it had already begun to mean to me. It was already clear that I was a part of a great legacy.

The question now was, what could I do to continue what God had already begun in the life of Daniel Blue?

I next wanted to see St. Andrews AME Church, the church Daniel Blue founded in his home in 1850. It was a Sacramento historical landmark that virtually no one knew about. Daniel Blue co-founded it

17

with the two Fletcher brothers, Barney and George, from Maryland. They purchased the land on 7th Street between G and H Streets for $250, built a twenty-foot by 30-foot wooden facility, and began meeting as a church with twenty-seven members. Because of the segregation laws in place, in 1854 they established a school for African American, Native American, Asian American and Latin American students.

On November 20, 1855, Daniel Blue and St. Andrews AME Church hosted the first State Convention of Colored Citizens of California. Delegates from ten Northern California counties gathered to discuss, one, the right to testify in court against whites; and two, the right to vote. The following year's convention was again held at St. Andrews AME Church, and they raised more than $20,000 to help support their lobbying campaign.

Then, for the 1857 Convention of Colored Citizens of California, they had to meet in San Francisco because the initial appeals presented to the state legislature were ignored. It would not be until 1863, after eight years of relentless campaigning, that the right to vote and the right to testify in court were awarded to African American citizens in California. Thanks to the political activism of Daniel Blue and St. Andrews AME Church, the State of California moved the needle a little further forward for the cause of equal rights.

In 1867, St. Andrews AME Church constructed a larger and more permanent brick building, one that served them well for over eighty years. St. Andrews then moved to a new location in 1951, at 2131 8th

Street, right across the street from Southside Park. That was the park my mother took Don and me to for Easter egg hunts when we were little boys. It was also the park where I was employed by the city of Sacramento as pool manager for more than six years, starting in college. Southside Park was also the same park where I did much of my training and preparation for playing college football.

How ironic that, for some of my life, I had played in front of that church and had run past it hundreds of times but had no idea it was a part of my own personal heritage, or that I was a part of its. Now, as I stood in front of the church and gazed across the street at the pool and park, I thought about how close I had been to all this family history and legacy and yet had no idea.

I began to wonder what my life might have looked like now if as a child I had known about the legacy of Daniel Blue. What choices or decisions would I have made differently? Would I have pursued other things? Where would I be if Daniel Blue had been able to pass on his wealth to me and my family? What kind of generational wealth and opportunities might I have missed? And what would I be doing? Oh, the many questions that bombarded my mind!

But the first and most intriguing question I pondered was, how did an African American man like Daniel Blue get from Kentucky to California more than two thousand miles away safely, unharmed, and unscathed in 1849? Those were very dangerous times for any man or woman, black or white. He would have had to deal with a myriad of challenges, uncharted territory, adverse weather, bandits, lawlessness, and bigotry at its highest levels. It was during this time that the west was truly the wild, wild west. So, how did he make it?

The answer to that question was discovered after about two years of searching by my dear friend and researcher, Robin Rositani, when she discovered who Daniel Blue's enslaver was. His name was Mason Doherty, an Irish immigrant who had a brother named John Doherty. It seems they caught gold fever in 1849 and devised a plan that would allow John to bring Daniel to California and mine for gold while Mason remained in Kentucky. If John and Daniel were successful in their search for gold, then Mason would come out west, as well. John Doherty and Daniel Blue arrived in Sacramento on September 2, 1849, by way of wagon train. The rest is the history that we were not taught in school.

Schools did not present to us the whole truth, only what some historians wanted us to know and believe. The facts are that California in the 1800s was a very dark, dangerous, and corrupt place, practically devoid of law. Many of the laws were bad because many of the civic leaders and politicians were crooked and greedy.

Peter Burnett, the first governor of California, was full of hatred. A racist, he hated blacks and Native Americans and helped to pass laws that called for the latter's extermination. In his petition to the United States government for California's admission into the Union, he claimed that California would be a slave-free state, yet he was a slaveowner with two slaves in his own house.

General John Sutter, credited for being the founder of Sacramento, was unsavory, as well. To gain and control 55,000 acres of land, he lied to both the Mexican and United States governments about his intended use of that land, actually using it to build a fort where he enslaved, raped, and murdered hundreds of the indigenous. He even went to Hawaii and brought back Hawaiians to enslave and sell.

Before the Gold Rush, California's population was around 160,000 people, of which 150,000 were Native American, about 6,500 were Mexicans, 1,500 were white, and the rest were various immigrants. By the end of the Gold Rush in 1859, the state's population had grown to 379,994 people, while the Native American population had fallen to about 30,000.

Before the Gold Rush began, there were less than 160 African American slaves in California. By the end of the Gold Rush, more than 2,000 African American slaves had been brought to California to mine for gold, mainly from Texas, Kentucky, Missouri, and Arkansas.

Corrupt men like Sutter and Burnett were glorified in California's history books and honored by having streets, schools, banks, and hospitals named after them, while good, selfless, and God-fearing men like Daniel Blue were left out of our recorded history. It's time that all of California's stories were told.

CHAPTER 2

DANIEL BLUE'S LEGACY

Throughout my search for significance, purpose, and legacy, and my discovery of Daniel Blue, I experienced several moments of being totally overwhelmed by emotion. One such moment happened on Thursday, May 4, 2023, at about 11:30 a.m., while shooting an historical segment in Sacramento, about the life of Daniel Blue for LeBron James's Springhill production company, at the Center for Sacramento History.

I was called into a room to rehearse when the center's senior archivist, Kim Hayden, wheeled in a cart with several large and very old leather-bound books. One of the books was labeled "Marriage A," and in it were the first and earliest records of couples married in Sacramento even before California became a state in 1850. Kim opened it to show me that Daniel Blue and Lucinda Luny were married on August 9, 1850, and were the second couple married in the city.

The magnitude of this historic discovery hit me like a ton of bricks, and right there, I lost it. I began to shed tears of frustration and confusion. I was proud, amazed, angry, and upset all over again, wondering why my ancestors were not included in the history books of Sacramento and California.

That day I also learned that Daniel Blue was selected to be a porter for the California State assembly in 1871; he was chosen to be the rear porter at the gubernatorial inauguration of Newton Booth in 1872; and in 1880, four years before his death, he was selected with other prominent Black citizens to greet U.S. President Rutherford B. Hayes, the first sitting president to travel west of the Rocky Mountains.

I was also able to find and read Daniel Blue's obituary, published in *The Sacramento Daily Union* on October 18, 1884, the day before his funeral. The full article below was pulled from the California Digital Newspaper Collection, UCR Center for Bibliographical Studies and Research (cdnc.ucr.edu)

An Old Man Gone

Daniel Blue, a colored citizen known to all the people of Sacramento, and who died suddenly this week in the 89th year of his age, was one of the most familiar figures on Sacramento streets for over a quarter of a century. He is to be buried tomorrow. For a Sacramentan to have said he did not know Uncle Daniel Blue was to argue his ignorance of the city and its people. Daniel

Blue was a slave in Kentucky until far into manhood's prime. He came to California in the earliest of her pioneer days, having been here over thirty-five years.

He was the founder and main stay of the African Methodist Episcopal Church in this city, and the most persistent solicitor for means to maintain it. What was especially noticeable, however, about Uncle Daniel was his native gentility. He greeted all men with a smile, and his countenance was radiant when it beamed upon children. For everyone he had a kind and a cheering word, and a graceful salute. His urbanity was not obsequious, nor his constant cheerfulness obtrusive. He was by nature a polite man, and though to manhood's prime lie was under the cloud of slavery, in his later years he was notably well informed, intelligent and able to hold his own upon all the living topics of the time. He could raise more money for his church than any other member. As one citizen put it yesterday, "There was not a house door in this city that did not open to the call of Uncle Daniel." Few men with such limited advantages so roundly tilled the measure of a peaceful life as this untutored but genial old man, whose countenance never frowned upon his fellows and whose life was one of sincere piety. The city will miss the familiar bent form of the old man, with his beaming countenance fringed with a beard of white; will miss the unstudied and graceful salute of Uncle Daniel; will miss the persuasive pleas for the church of his heart; will miss the benedictions he ministered to old and young and middle-aged. It will miss the kindly old negro man, who lived up to his highest development, passed the allotted lease of life without a shade of querulous old age, and went to his rest known of all his fellow-citizens, and with fewer to speak ill of him than falls to the lot of most men.

The following Saturday, May 6, 2023, I had the privilege to share a bit of Daniel Blue's legacy of love and his fight for human rights during a public hearing before the California Reparations Task Force Committee at Mills College in Oakland, California. After nearly two years of research and investigation, the California Task Force Committee was preparing to make its final recommendations concerning reparations for the state's African Americans to Governor Gavin Newsom and the state legislature. I have no idea how the recommendations will be considered or acted upon by the governor, the legislature, and the people of California.

What I do know is that there was an enslaved man named Daniel Blue, born on March 1, 1796, in Monroe County, Kentucky, who arrived on a wagon train in Sacramento, California, on September 2, 1849. He was an amazing man who influenced Sacramento and California history and lived a remarkable life helping others. He discovered gold and changed the landscape of his new state by founding the first and oldest African American church west of the Mississippi River, as well as a school for minority students, all while organizing and leading efforts to get laws passed that would allow African Americans in California the privilege to vote and the right to testify against whites in court. Most importantly, before he died on October 15, 1884, he ended slavery in the state of California in 1864 by freeing an enslaved and abused twelve-year-old girl named Edith, the last known slave in California.

CHAPTER 3

MY BEGINNING

Dr. Billy Graham once said, "The greatest legacy one can pass on to one's children, and grandchildren is not money or other material things accumulated in one's life, but rather a legacy of character and faith."

I believe the story of my search for significance, purpose and legacy began at the tender age of three, way back in 1959. That's when I, Lester Robinson III, the first-born child of Lester and Janet Robinson, remember being formally introduced to Jesus Christ at church. Those were good times, sweet days of innocence and bliss. Back then, gas cost about twenty-three cents a gallon, the average price of a new house was $12,400, Fidel Castro had just seized power in Cuba, "Rawhide" and "Bonanza" were big hits on television, and Barbie had just become a doll.

It was during this time, too, that I was taken to Mother Berry's Sunday School class for toddlers, ages three through five, at Christ Temple Apostolic Church, which was then located at 1619 R Street in downtown Sacramento. Christ Temple Apostolic Church was founded by Pastor Thomas Holman in 1915 and was now under the leadership of his son, District Elder Robert B. Holman, Sr. Elder Holman was an extremely passionate follower of Jesus Christ and desired to experience the manifest power of God in every way mentioned in the Bible. Along with great passion, he had a massive heart for serving and caring for God's people. His Christian walk was one of extreme honesty, integrity, and humility. "Brother Bob," as we lovingly called him, taught us the uncompromised Word of God.

Christ Temple Apostolic Church was in the south end of downtown Sacramento and sat on the railroad tracks. Just across the street was a large, cement, ice and storage house where trains would stop daily and exchange all kinds of frozen goods. It was on these same railroad tracks that I used to race with the other young boys of my church over and over again, which helped develop the amazing gift of speed and acceleration that God would later use to get me into all the right places.

The building located at 1619 R Street was what the old timers called "The Hole" because, back in 1935, it was dug out as a basement for a church to be built on, but for some reason it was never completed. Back then, when you entered the church, you stepped into a small vestibule and then made an immediate right turn and descended two flights of stairs into a large cement room that served as our place of worship.

This building may have been called "The Hole," but in this place, I witnessed the power of God move in ways I could never have imagined and have not seen or experienced since. In "The Hole," I saw crippled people leave walking. I saw demons cast out of people. I even saw the dead rise. In this place of worship, I saw many lives dramatically transformed.

For years to come, "The Hole" influenced, shaped, and transformed my life in many ways. In this hallowed place, I was set on a wonderful spiritual course. There, I was discipled and mentored by the seasoned older men and mothers of our church, who taught us how to fear and reverence God. I learned how to fast, pray, and trust in the Lord for every need I would ever have.

At 1619 R Street, I was trained to be a light, an example, and a real ambassador of Jesus Christ. It was here that I was taught the Word of God, from Genesis to Revelation. I was baptized here and became a Bible scholar, teacher, musician, and licensed minister of the Gospel.

Because of the foundation of strong Bible teachings, a daily commitment to fasting and prayer, and a tremendous devotion to the Bible and the application of its words, the tangible presence of the Holy Spirit was experienced in nearly every service. People came each week with a spirit of expectancy: expecting a word, a miracle, or a personal touch from God Almighty.

It was in this warm and loving spiritual incubator that Mother Berry, a short, beautiful, light- skinned, African American woman of about 80 years old, with no wrinkles and a long, silver, braided ponytail that almost touched the floor, taught me my first Bible lesson from a small 3 x 5 Sunday School card.

I will never forget it. The lesson was from Revelation 3:20 (KJV), where Jesus says,

"Behold, I stand at the door, and knock: if any man hear my voice, and open the door, I will come into him, and will sup with him, and he with me."

This verse and the picture on the card showing Jesus knocking at the door of someone's heart intrigued me and left an indelible impression on me. The message of God wanting to have a relationship with me, and its significance was reinforced because, later that afternoon at home, my mother discussed and reviewed the Sunday School lesson with me. I was so touched by its message, I wanted to know more about Jesus. I wanted to be His friend, and I wanted Him to be mine. For some unexplainable reason, I felt the nudge of the Holy Spirit that made me want to do something special, something significant with my life for Him.

It was as if God had given me, at this early age, a personal invitation and made a special connection with me, one that made me want to trust Him, be close to Him, and know more about Him. Even then, I felt that somehow I was being chosen to be a part of something exciting and special that He was doing. If I had been asked at that time to give my life to Jesus, I know that I would have said yes. I didn't know it then, but I believe that this day, when I had this first personal encounter with Jesus, was the beginning of my lifelong search for significance, purpose, and legacy.

CHAPTER 4

I GOT A "C"

I don't remember my mother or father ever addressing racism or hatred in our home. They taught us by their words and actions to love everyone. I saw them share food and money with anyone who asked for or needed it. I saw them take in people who needed a place to stay. I saw them on a regular basis give to others without prompting or reservation.

My parents truly lived out the scripture at St. Matthew 22:39 that says we should love our neighbors as ourselves. God seemed to always be at the center of what my parents said and did and, as a result, our house was a popular place to hang out. Friends and neighbors knew they could always come to the Robinson house and enjoy good food, fun, and laughter.

But amid all the fun and activity, I always felt a little different. I felt like I was experiencing life from a different perspective than others. Sometimes I felt as if I really didn't belong, as if I was just passing through. I was present, alert, and engaged, but at times I felt like a voyeur, just spectating and taking notice of people and things.

I remember one particular childhood experience and the effect it had on me. I know that this one experience altered the trajectory of my entire life. It affected and changed my attitude and approach concerning my goals and expectations in life from that point forward.

Everything changed for me when I got a C on my report card.

I was in the fourth grade at Riverside Elementary School. Riverside Elementary was located on the west side of Sacramento, in a community known as Land Park, a very nice neighborhood where mostly upwardly mobile families lived. Most of these people came from old money. I say "old money" because these families had lived in this neighborhood for several generations. They were afforded opportunities that enabled them to pass generational wealth on to their children and grandchildren. The homes in the Land Park area were beautiful and very well built, typically with well-kept and manicured lawns and beautiful landscaping. Most of these homes were not owned by people of color.

Redlining is the systematic denial of various federal and local agency services that discriminated against people of color by refusing or limiting their access to preferable geographical areas that could be secured through favorable loans to secure them. Redlining was in full effect in Sacramento during the 1960s. I believe my parents were able to secure our home in Land Park because my great-grandmother, Hazel

White, Daniel Blue's granddaughter, was a very fair skinned African American who could pass for white.

We lived in a very nice, three-bedroom, two-story home, with a detached two car garage and a large backyard that included a patio and swimming pool. Not to mention, my father drove a new, large, beautiful Cadillac. Looking back, I came to realize that not many African Americans enjoyed that lifestyle in the early 1960s. We were living a blessed life and, of course, I had no idea that we were. I was born into what we had and that was all I knew.

Land Park had very few minorities. As a matter of fact, my brother Don, another boy named Harold, his sister, and I were the only African Americans in the whole school. Most of the students at Riverside Elementary were either white or Asian.

Students at Riverside Elementary came ready and were eager to learn. They were articulate, clean, immaculately dressed, and always had nice haircuts and hairstyles as if they had just fallen out of a Macy's catalog. The campus grounds were very orderly, calm, and clean.

My fourth-grade teacher was Mrs. Bay. She was young and attractive with pretty green eyes, and I had a little schoolboy crush on her. I was doing pretty well in school at this point, but I was shy and relatively quiet probably because I was the only black kid in my class. I typically paid attention and listened fairly well when I wasn't daydreaming or watching the squirrels play in the oak trees or on the power lines. Because I had a good memory, I normally tested well. I had always managed to score either As or Bs, but, for some reason, during this semester, I got a C in science.

I had never received a C before, but it didn't matter much to me because I knew that a C was average and, to me, that wasn't bad. I was somewhere in the middle of the class in terms of rank and that was okay. At least that is what I thought.

On the day report cards were given out, I carried mine home, gave it to my mother as usual, and then went outside to play with my siblings. Later that evening when my father got home from work, he carefully inspected our report cards and it soon became apparent that he was not pleased, especially with mine. He called me into the living room to have a conversation. He told me how disappointed he was that I had received a C and that he knew I could do better. I, of course, countered that my siblings had received Cs as well and asked him why he wasn't making a big deal with them.

I really couldn't understand my father's train of thinking. It wasn't fair and just didn't make sense to me. He shared with me that he felt I could do much better in science. He said it was my job to do my very best in school because I was the oldest and he expected me to set a good example for my younger siblings.

He then told me that he was going to give me a spanking. A spanking? For what? Just because I got a C? I kept thinking I shouldn't be spanked because I got an average grade in science. I hated spankings.

Nevertheless, because I knew the spanking was coming, I was in a state of sheer torment for the rest of the day. I tried to take my time washing the dishes that night hoping my father would be too tired and fall asleep. But there would be no such luck for me.

At six foot three and about 220 pounds, my father was a pretty good-sized man. He had a large, thick, black leather belt that was about three inches wide, and he believed in using it. Later that evening, he made good on his word and gave me a spanking. I was so mad, I didn't even cry. I was angry, hurt, and confused.

I was so upset about the punishment that I asked to speak with my dad again. I really wanted him to know how I felt. I explained to him that I was sorry and never meant to disappoint him, but I still thought it was unfair that I got a spanking for getting a C. In the moments that followed that exchange, my dad grabbed me by my shoulders, looked me directly in the eyes and, after pausing briefly, said seven words that I would remember for the rest of my life: "Son, you can't afford to be average."

At the time, I didn't understand what he was saying or what he meant, but I never forgot those words. I would not be anywhere near average in anything for the rest of my life. Those words were cemented in my brain, my heart, and my character.

Growing up as a young African American man in America, I came to fully understand the truth and validity of my father's words. I learned I had to be much better than my white peers in order to have any chance of achieving success in America.

I didn't know at the time that one day very soon, we would leave Riverside Elementary School, our nice home, and the beautiful neighborhood of Land Park. But God would use the memory of Riverside, and the Land Park neighborhood to serve as motivation for my survival later.

CHAPTER 5

FROM LAND PARK TO OAK PARK

In the late spring of 1965, near the end of my fourth-grade school year, my life took a drastic turn. The world was literally turned upside down and inside out. The United States entered the Vietnam War. Malcolm X was shot dead in New York. Dr. Martin Luther King Jr., was leading a civil rights march in Selma, Alabama, and race riots were breaking out in Watts, California.

During these turbulent times, because of financial and marital problems, my family had to move from the nice, prosperous, and safe side of town, Land Park, to the not so nice, dangerous side of town, which was a neighborhood called "Oak Park."

OAK PARK

In Oak Park, everything I knew changed and I began to see the world from a much different perspective. Talk about culture shock! It was a tremendous culture shock! Until this time, I had lived in a very nice, safe, and sheltered world, where everything and everybody seemed safe, pleasant, and positive. In Land Park, I had never experienced any real fear, violence, or discomfort, I had never heard a curse word or seen drugs or alcohol unless it was on television or at the movies. But when we moved to Oak Park, such things were as real as real could get. It was an introduction to the real world on the other side of town.

Looking back, the first thing I remember about Oak Park was that our house didn't have a fireplace, a den, a big backyard, or a patio or swimming pool, and there were no sidewalks on the streets, just ditches. I also noticed that at night the streets were very dark because there were no streetlights.

OAKRIDGE ELEMENTARY SCHOOL

I will never forget my first day at Oakridge Elementary School. We had moved to Oak Park late in the school year, with only about three to four weeks left to complete. I had to walk to school as usual, probably only about a mile or so, but when I got there, I immediately noticed how different it was. It felt much different than Riverside Elementary School. These kids seemed unaware that they were sent to school to learn and prepare for life.

Oakridge was depressing, dirty, and dreary. There were fights almost daily. Either the students were fighting with each other, or some parent was on campus threatening or trying to fight a teacher or administrator. This school wasn't a place that made me feel safe, hopeful, or excited about the future. It felt more like I was hopelessly lost or trapped in a jungle or prison. It seemed like the most important thing to do here was to survive the daily, non-stop drama. I noticed that most of the kids on campus weren't dressed well and didn't speak well. They were not friendly; they were very aggressive and didn't smile much. Most of them seemed either angry or afraid.

I clearly remember there were more African American kids than I had ever seen together at any time at school. There were also quite a few Hispanic kids, but very few white kids, and they always seemed afraid.

During the afternoon recess, I was minding my own business, just walking around the playground and checking things out, when this big black kid walked up to me and called me a punk, and, of course, everyone started laughing. I didn't know what a punk was because I had never heard the word before, but I did know it wasn't anything good because of the way everyone reacted. I guess because I was small and articulate and dressed differently, he assumed I was someone he could bully and have fun with. After everyone stopped laughing, I told the boy I wasn't a punk. He quickly replied, "Yes, you are!" and then he pushed me real hard in the chest, causing me to stumble backwards. In my head I said, *Oh, No, he didn't!* I immediately countered with a barrage of punches and kicks and before he knew it, I had him down on the ground on his back with me on his chest beating him in the face.

I remember hearing a lot of the kids running over and shouting "Fight! Fight! Oh, a Fight!" and "Kick his ass! Kick his ass!" They were laughing and cheering as if we were the entertainment for the day. It wasn't long before several of the yard duty teachers pulled us apart and took us to the principal's office.

On the way, I was nervous because I had never been to the principal's office for fighting and I knew my father was going to be called and told what happened. I also knew he was going to whip my butt when he got home from work. Because my father was a devout Christian, he didn't believe in fighting, and he wanted my brother Don and I to act like Christians, as well. He wanted us to follow the Bible teachings and turn the other cheek. My father didn't know it, but I didn't believe in turning the other cheek, so that wasn't happening!

When we arrived at the principal's office, the bell rang to signal the end of recess and a few minutes later, which seemed like forever, the principal came in and asked us what happened. I explained that the other boy approached me and started everything. I told him how he had called me a punk twice and pushed me hard in the chest, so I had to defend myself and fight.

I might as well have been talking to the wall. That principal didn't even listen. He didn't care one bit. He didn't care about who was wrong or right. He didn't care about using this opportunity to teach us about values or correct behavior. He didn't care that I was much smaller than the other boy, or that this was my first day on campus. He acted more like a warden than a principal. He just wanted to discipline us and get us out of there.

After we each told him what happened, he promptly announced that the penalty for fighting at Oakridge Elementary School was a two-day suspension and three swats from his paddle. His paddle was a large, thick, wooden paddle used to play wall ball, except it had been altered with three one-inch holes drilled into the center of it to cause more pain. Then, with a big smile on his face, he announced that it was time for us to receive our swats. He asked us who wanted to go first, and I chose to go last so that I could see what these swats would look and sound like.

As the principal prepared to swat the other boy, he made light of the situation by blowing on the paddle and dusting it off on his pants as if he was shining it up. He seemed to take great pleasure in instructing us to bend over and grab our ankles. He then started to swing away on us as if he were chopping down an oak tree. Those paddle swats stung bad, but I was so angry, I didn't make a sound or shed a tear.

On the long walk home, I was totally consumed in thought about what I would tell my mother. I was thinking about what she might say and about how my father was going to whip my butt for fighting. I was almost home from school when I saw what I thought was a mountain lion staring at me from the roof of our neighbor's house. I did a double take and sure enough it was a mountain lion! Minute by minute and day by day, it was becoming crystal clear that this new neighborhood was not Land Park but more like the wild, wild west! I looked down at the ground and in the dirt I saw many large paw prints.

That was enough for me to run as fast as I could the rest of the way home. When I stepped inside our house, my mother asked why I was so out of breath, and I told her about the mountain lion on our neighbor's roof. Of course, she didn't believe me and laughed it off. I tried to convince her that I really did see a mountain lion, but she just dismissed it as my imagination gone wild.

Then, my mother asked me why I was home from school so early. When I shared with her what happened that morning, to my surprise she smiled and said she was so proud I defended myself and that it would be our little secret. She promised me that she would not tell my father.

Later that week, my mother saw the mountain lion for herself, causing all of us to wonder why anyone would have a mountain lion as a pet in a residential area. A month later, the couple that lived next door moved away and we never saw the mountain lion again.

After living for about two months in this new house, we moved to another house, an even older Victorian-styled house on 2nd Avenue, deeper in the heart of Oak Park. It was while living in this house that I first witnessed true cold-blooded violence. It happened on a very hot summer day, already nearing one hundred degrees at only 10:00 in the morning. My brother Don and a couple of friends and I were on our way to Oak Park's swimming pool at McClatchy Park. As we walked through Oak Park, we passed by several crap games that the men young and old were playing under large evergreen trees on patches of dirt that had been worn away in the grass from the countless craps games played on them. As we weaved our way through, we came upon two men talking, one of whom was an older black man wearing a long tweed trench coat. They were standing directly ahead of me about six feet away.

All of a sudden, the man in the trench coat pulled out a gun, a revolver, and emptied it—*Bang! Bang! Bang! Bang! Bang!*—into the other man at point blank range. He then casually put the gun back in his coat pocket and calmly walked away as if nothing ever happened. I stopped in my tracks. It happened so fast and so matter-of-factly that it didn't look, sound, or feel real. It looked fake. But, unfortunately, it wasn't. The gun was real. The bullets were real. The shooter was real. The victim was real. And so was his death.

At that moment, my friends walking behind me pushed me forward and said to just keep going and not say anything. In the park, we learned how to do two things very quickly. One was not to talk about any of the terrible things you saw, and two was not to show your emotions. It was much safer for you not to say anything or show anything. Later that evening as we left the pool, we found out that the men had been arguing about who caught a fish. It was like the wild, wild west in Oak Park. A man got killed over a freakin' fish!

DONNER ELEMENTARY SCHOOL

By the time school started in September, we had moved again to another rundown house in Oak Park, on San Jose Way. This house was so rat- and roach-infested that it was later condemned as unsafe by the City of Sacramento.

On San Jose Way, my life continued to change because of things I saw and experienced. Also, during this time, I saw less and less of my father and spending more and more time in the streets.

We were now enrolled at Donner Elementary School. At Donner, there were lots of kids because there were lots of families, big families. That meant that activity on the playground during recess and physical education classes was very competitive.

Competition had always been a big part of my life. My brother Don is ten months younger than me but for the majority of my life he's been taller than me. As young kids, we were always pitted against each other by family and friends in running, wrestling or whatever. Our church had a very large group of young people and everything we did there— from Bible games to singing, playing instruments to racing alongside the railroad tracks after church—was very, very competitive.

One day at Donner Elementary, as I was coming out of class for recess, I heard this kid say that Lynn Lewis was the fastest person in the school and that she was even beating the boys. I told him she was not the fastest and that I could beat her. Of course, he argued that I couldn't beat her because, to him, I was just little black Lester who couldn't do anything because I was a small, black nerd. Back in the early Sixties, being black or very dark-skinned wasn't cool, nor was it fun. The kids made fun of me and called me every black name they could think of: Tar Baby, Blackie, Little Black Sambo, the Creature from the Black Lagoon, Black Chip, and Charcoal. None of those names mattered much to me right then because I knew I could beat Lynn Lewis running. I knew I could beat her because a year before we moved to Oak Park, my mom often babysat her, and we would race in the backyard, and I beat her all the time.

When I made it to the playground, sure enough, Lynn was out there on the grass, with her long legs and no shoes on, just socks, beating everyone she raced. So, the next time they all lined up to race, I took off my shoes, lined up right next to her, and left her in the dust! The kids on the playground looked at me in amazement, because I had just smoked Lynn Lewis. I went back over to the boy who said I couldn't run to say I told you so. I also let him know that my brother Don could beat her, too.

That day, things changed drastically for the Robinson brothers. Once word got out that we could run, the older boys in the neighborhood and their younger brothers began stopping by our house on Thursday nights to take us to the teen center.

At the teen center, the youth staff and the older boys taught us how to play competitive team sports, like basketball and football. Soon, I was invited to run in a track meet for the Sacramento City Parks and Recreation team representing Oak Park. The City Championship Track and Field Finals Meet was a night track meet held at Hughes Stadium. We were signed up to compete in the 4 x 100-yard relay, and something special happened that night: we set a new world record for our age group.

THE SODA TRUCK

As far as education was concerned, the first two years of school in Oak Park were a total waste. During my fifth and sixth grade years, my reading comprehension level was so much higher than the other kids in my class that a typical day at school for me was to spend the morning with my class and then after lunch I was sent to the library to read the Metro page of the *Sacramento Union* and then had to write an essay about what I read. Needless to say, school for me became pretty boring.

Across the street from Donner Elementary School was a supermarket called State Fair Market. Every Tuesday just before morning recess, the soda truck came to replenish the store's supply of sodas. From our classroom windows, we could see when it pulled up and parked in the back alley. When it arrived, a whispered chorus of "Soda Truck!" spread among students, alerting all those who were interested.

The soda trucks back in the late 1960s were open and uncovered, so if you wanted to, you could just snatch a six-pack or two of bottled sodas off the truck and walk away. Just about every Tuesday, during the morning recess, a group of us left campus and ran to the alley to raid the truck. We grabbed one or two six-packs at a time, sprinted down the alley, and then returned to campus.

Once we made it back to school, we used the chain-link fence brackets to pry open the bottles, then quickly drank the sodas and returned to class. In those days, there were no free lunch programs at school. We were wrong, and we knew it. Most of us were from large, impoverished families, and we were hungry. A group of us stole food for lunch on a regular basis for nearly two years.

At first, stealing was hard for me, and I felt guilty, because I knew better. I clearly knew right from wrong, and I was wrong. I was attending church, going to Sunday School, and hearing the Word of God several times every week, but when it came time to make choices, I made the bad ones. I had totally succumbed to peer pressure, and now I was just going along with the crowd. I was on the edge of ruining my life now that I was part of the cool crowd, heading in the wrong direction and making a lot of poor decisions on a regular basis.

It was almost as if I didn't care. I justified the bad choices by telling myself I was young, black, and poor, and nobody cared. The truth is that I should have been caught, arrested, and put in juvenile hall or, even worse, jailed for a lot of the things I was doing. It was only because of the mercy and grace of God that I never was caught. When I think back on those times, I know God protected me because my mother was praying for me, and He had a much better plan for my life.

Prior to our move from Land Park to Oak Park, I noticed that my mother and father had begun to argue more frequently and longer and louder. There were now six children in our family: myself, Don, twins Shevonne and Shaunielle, my baby brother Stephan, and my baby

49

sister Celine. Looking back now at where my parents might have been in terms of stress, is alarming.

My mother was a stay-at-home mom with six kids and not much help at all because my father was now working two jobs. He worked for the State of California during the day and at the U.S. Postal Service Office at night. Their stress levels must have been through the roof because they both liked nice things.

My mother liked very nice clothes. I 'm talking expensive dresses, suits, hats, shoes, and furs. My dad had very expensive taste in clothes, as well. When it came to cars, he was very fond of Cadillacs and Lincolns. As a result of the great financial stress fueled by their love of nice things along with other problems, my parents eventually divorced.

Because I was the oldest child, their divorce was probably the hardest on me. I secretly began to act out. No one knew it, but I started to hang out more with some of the rougher neighborhood kids. My father had forbidden those kinds of associations and had kept a very close eye on my choice of friends when he was around. But he was gone now, and my mother was overwhelmed with the task of raising all of us alone, equipped with only a third-grade education and government assistance.

At twelve years old, I started Peter Lassen Junior High and had to walk nearly five miles to get to school. The summer before I started, someone had burned down Stanford Junior High School which was just around the corner from our house. That walk to Peter Lassen was long and time consuming and I soon hated it enough to start skipping school. I hung out at the park, the bowling alley, or Kmart. Some of the other neighborhood boys and I would smoke cigarettes and, when we could get it, weed. If we got really bored, we sometimes hotwired and stole cars. In the seventh grade, I was getting almost straight Fs, and no one seemed to know or even care. I missed my father terribly and I needed the accountability that he had demanded of me. I was failing on all levels.

Then one day when I actually went to school, my counselor, Mrs. Braxton, called me into her office. She was a nicely but conservatively dressed, middle-aged black woman, and she got in my face good.

"Mr. Robinson, what is wrong with you?" she said. "You've been missing a lot of school, and when you do come, you're late. I don't understand this because I'm looking at your records from elementary school and you were almost a straight A student. I want you to know that this is unacceptable, and I am going to be watching you. I want you to join the track team and the choir, and the next time I see you, I want to see you on the honor roll. Do you understand me, young man?"

I don't know if Mrs. Braxton knew it, but she saved me and redirected my life. She literally rescued me. She was one of the angels God strategically placed in my path to help straighten me out. I did join the choir and the track team, and by the end of the school year I was back on the honor roll. It's remarkable how a little attention, challenge, and follow-up from an adult can positively affect a child.

THE JACKET AND THE CHIP

In ninth grade, I decided I was going to try out for the flag football team at Peter Lassen. I felt good about my chances because, for one, I had already been a part of several City of Sacramento Parks and Recreation championship teams. Two, I had great quickness, good hands, and a high football IQ. And three, I was in last period P.E. class where all the top athletes were, and I was one of the best. In this class is where I earned the camaraderie and respect of most of the other top athletes in the school.

I not only loved the game of football and wanted to play, but I had a jacket on my back that I needed to get off and I needed to get it off in a big way, and playing football was a good way to do it. It was about this time that my father and mother split up and got divorced.

It was also during this time that my father was accused of being gay. I was angry, conflicted, and confused that the man I loved, respected, and idolized was gay. How could my dad be gay? How could a man have a wife, six kids, be a popular church leader, and be gay? I was his first-born child, his first son, and named after him, and I wasn't gay. I felt people would somehow look at me as his son and wonder if I was gay, too, and I wasn't having that. The kids from the neighborhood and church were starting to talk and tease.

As a result of this revelation about my dad and the inner turmoil it caused for me, I became very sensitive and consequently had a bevy of fights. Back in the early Sixties, there was no such thing as gay tolerance. If you were gay, you were done. You were attacked, ostracized, excommunicated, and blacklisted. I not only wanted to make this team and play football, but I also desperately needed to convince everyone that I was a man and not a gay one.

After two weeks of tryouts, which I felt went very well, the cut list went up on the wall in the boy's gym, and I was on it. I could not believe I got cut. I was angry, shocked, and embarrassed because lots of guys who made the team I could beat in any phase of the game. Many of those who made the cut were surprised that I didn't. It had to be a mistake. Perhaps they were in a hurry and put my name on the list by accident? I needed to know, so I went into the coach's office and asked for an explanation, because I just knew I should have made that team.

The coach said he thought I was too small. How could he say that? Why did he say that? It was flag football, which is all about speed, quickness, allusiveness, and good ball skills, all of which I possessed. I asked him how he could cut me when he had kept so many guys on the team that I could clearly beat.

Experiencing that cut and missing the opportunity to prove myself as a man while having to watch my friends play football and go undefeated to win the city championship without me that year, put a chip on my shoulder the size of Mount Everest. That experience and those words, "I just think you're too small," ignited within me enough anger and passion to play football for the rest of my life. The very next week, I went to Kmart and bought a one-hundred-and-forty-pound weight set and pushed it five miles in a shopping cart all the way home. I began training like a maniac for my sophomore year of football in high school.

CHAPTER 6

1969

It was now 1969 and in the neighborhood, the top music hits were "Mother Popcorn" by James Brown, "My Cherie Amour" by Stevie Wonder, "It's Your Thing" by The Isley Brothers, and "I Can't Get Next to You" by The Temptations. "Broadway Joe" Namath and the New York Jets defeated the Baltimore Colts sixteen to seven at the Orange Bowl in Super Bowl Three, the Boeing 747 completed its first commercial flight, Richard M. Nixon succeeded Lyndon B. Johnson to become the thirty-seventh president of the United States, James Earl Ray pled guilty to the murder of Dr. Martin Luther King Jr., Sirhan Sirhan was convicted of killing Senator Robert F. Kennedy, and Neil Armstrong became the first man to walk on the moon. America and the world were becoming very aggressive, very restless, and very violent.

In Oak Park, because of racial tension, the lack of education, the lack of opportunity, rising inflation, and the economic decline it caused, the poverty and frustration levels were accelerating fast and criminal activity, such as drug dealing, burglary, and prostitution were commonplace. In the middle of all this social, political, and economic unrest were the Black Muslims, the Black Panthers, and the police. I crossed paths with each of these groups in one way or another.

THE BLACK PANTHERS

About that time, some young black men began showing up in the neighborhood, wearing black berets and calling themselves the Black Panthers. They were doing lots of good things to assist the residents of the Oak Park community, like cleaning up junk-filled yards, helping the elderly and needy with food, and helping people get legal and tax assistance. They also picked up kids like my brother Don and me and brought us to the Black Panther Party offices to feed us breakfast, and then they took us to school. But things also started getting pretty crazy in "the park" around that time.

THE RIOTS

On Sunday, July 15, 1969, I got up early and rode the church bus to Christ Temple Apostolic Church on R Street in downtown Sacramento. After church, I invited a friend over to our house for dinner. Our plan was to eat, play some basketball, and then, at 6:00 p.m., return to church for youth service.

Back then, 35th Street in Oak Park was very nice. It was like a small downtown plaza, with lots of thriving restaurants, apparel shops, department stores, gift shops, banks, and bars. The Sacramento

Regional Transit buses and trolley cars traveled up and down the street filled with patrons and shoppers.

After dinner, we walked to Oak Park to play basketball as planned. We were having a great time laughing and talking smack to one another when suddenly, we looked up and saw police paddy wagons and cars driving through the park and headed in our direction at top speed. The officers were wearing white helmets and riot gear. I had never seen them dressed this way before.

Right about then, I heard a loud voice shouting out some kind of command through a megaphone, and then they started shooting at us! It was crazy! I couldn't believe it! They were *shooting* at us! For what reason I don't know, but we weren't waiting around to find out. We immediately dropped the basketball and sprinted as fast as we could to a chain-link fence about fifty yards away. I could feel the wind of bullets whizzing by me as I ran. We somehow got to the fence, hit it hard, flipped ourselves over, and ran home, jumping over backyard fences in a series of short cuts we knew in the neighborhood.

When we made it home, I told my mother what had happened. She was shocked and very upset. She immediately prayed, thanking God for getting us home safely and asking for his continued protection.

The next day, Monday, July 16th, a full-fledged riot broke out in Oak Park, starting right there on 35th Street, between the police and residents. I remember many of the buildings and shops were burnt down by fire from Molotov cocktails. I also heard that the Black Panther Party offices were shot up and many residents had been shot. The rumor was that the riots started because some residents were double parking on 5th Avenue and 35th Street, blocking traffic, and when the police showed up to stop it, people began throwing rocks at them.

Not long after the riots, all the nice stores, shops, businesses, and buses left and 35th Street became dark and desolate. I never found out the real reason why the riots happened or why the police were shooting at us. All I know is that the riots happened. I was there. It happened and, miraculously, we survived it.

Reflecting on these events and other experiences in my life, I can see how God was ever present, leading, loving, and protecting me even in Oak Park, the wild, wild west.

Not many months after that summer and the riots, I began to seriously think about the future, my life, and what I wanted to do with it. I really didn't have a firm plan of what I wanted to do or be, all I knew was that I wanted to do something meaningful and important. I wanted to be a part of something that was bigger than me. I wanted to do something truly significant with my life.

At the same time, I was very concerned that I wouldn't be able to achieve the desires in my heart because I was a young, black kid living in Oak Park without the benefit of a father, a leader, a guide, or a mentor. I was saying within myself and crying out to God in prayer,

God, I need Your help. I am lost. I don't have a father, and no one knows who I am. I don't have the benefit of a father's support, connections, friendships, or relationships. I have no one to teach me or help me. My mother can't even help me. She needs my help. I'm just a kid who has no idea how I am going to achieve significance. God, will You please help me?

One day, as I was reading the Bible, I landed in the book of Proverbs. Proverbs drew my attention because I had heard that it's writer, King Solomon, was the wisest man to ever live. When I opened to chapter one, I read verses one through four, which say (NLT):

These are the proverbs of Solomon, David's son, king of Israel;

Their purpose is to teach people wisdom and discipline, to help them understand the insights of the wise.

Their purpose is to teach people to live disciplined and successful lives, to help them do what is right, just, and fair.

These proverbs will give insight to the simple, knowledge and discernment to the young,
—Proverbs 1:1-4

I knew even at this age, because of my situation, that if I were to have any chance of living a successful life, I needed to acquire wisdom to make decisions that would lead to my success. Because the book of Proverbs promised to give subtilty to the simple and knowledge and discretion to the young man, I kept reading it, seeking to understand life, the world, myself, and God.

While reading, I discovered Proverbs 18:16 (KJV), a verse that intrigued, encouraged, and gave me hope for much of my life. It says,

> *"A man's gift makes room for him, and brings him before great men."*

I don't know why this scripture touched me the way it did, but it became my favorite verse and secret meditation. It made me feel confident. It didn't matter about the circumstance or the odds. I always had this feeling that if I worked hard at the gifts God gave me, He would allow someone to see me, like me, and make a way for me. It was like I had this secret pact with God, so I continued to work hard at doing my very best while looking to Him to provide opportunities.

CHAPTER 7

HIGH SCHOOL DAZE

In 1971, the voting age in the U.S. was lowered to 18. Walt Disney World had just opened in Orlando, Florida. The average American annual income was about $10,600. The average monthly rent was $150. Gas was forty cents a gallon, and a movie ticket cost a dollar fifty. The top movies were "Fiddler on the Roof," "Dirty Harry," and "Shaft." The top hit songs on the radio were "What's Going On" by Marvin Gaye, "It's Too Late" by Carole King, and "Spanish Harlem" by Aretha Franklin. And I started attending Sacramento High School, home of the mighty Dragons.

At the end of the year, the varsity football head coach at Sacramento High School, Dave Hotel, came to Peter Lassen Junior High to tell us about football there and to recruit for the team. Sac High was known for producing great athletes and had sent several of them to the NFL via the then Pacific Eight (Pac-8) Conference. At that time, there were two former Sac High Dragons from the neighborhood who had just made it to the NFL: Artimus "Tee" Parker, who held the interception record at USC and was now playing safety for the Philadelphia Eagles; and Leland Glass, who played wide receiver at the University of Oregon with quarterback Dan Fouts and was now playing with the Green Bay Packers.

Sometimes called "Big Daddy Dave," Coach Hotel loved speed and made it known to us that those who were skilled and could run fast would get lots of opportunities at Sac High. That summer, I reported to my first football practice at Sac High with a great sense of excitement and anticipation because I had speed.

COACH DELOACH

The junior varsity football coach was Gerald Deloach, himself a former football star at Sac High. He had received a full ride football scholarship to UC Davis and was drafted in the seventh round of the NFL draft in 1971 by the Oakland Raiders. Unfortunately, his NFL career ended abruptly when he suffered a career-ending knee injury. He then returned home to Sacramento to pursue his love of teaching and to coach at Sac High.

Gerald Deloach was a big guy, about six-feet-five inches tall and 285 pounds, and he was fast. He was the first big guy I had ever seen run that fast, so he had all my attention. Because he was my first head football coach, he would play a major role in developing my character as an athlete and a man.

Coach Deloach was a great role model for many of us young men who didn't have fathers. He was articulate, intelligent, and kind, but he was also a very intense guy when the situation called for it. He always spoke right to you, and he did not pull punches. What made him so special to me was that I knew he believed in me as a player and a person. It was Coach Deloach who gave me my first official coaching job when I returned to Sacramento after college. He hired me at John F. Kennedy High School as his running back/defensive back coach for the junior varsity football team in 1980. That same year, he also asked me to be his sprint coach for the track and field team, and the following year, he recommended me to the athletic director as his successor as the head track and field coach. I will forever be indebted to him for the opportunities he gave me and the great deposits of wisdom he made in my life.

When I began playing football, I wanted to play quarterback. So, I developed and possessed both the skills and the mentality to play the position very well. I was smart, I had a good arm, and a good understanding of the game, along with my exceptional quickness.

But unfortunately, I never played a single down as a quarterback in high school. A month before practices began, my best friend, Raymond Ware, advised me to change positions and play defensive back. He felt that I wouldn't get a fair shot at QB because it would probably go to Jim Breech, who was white and had a father on the city council. Raymond was my football mentor and best friend, so I listened to what he said and tried out for defensive back.

Even though I was one of the smallest players on the team, I ended up starting at strong cornerback. It was the perfect position for me because I was smart and tenacious, and the lifelong competitor in me enjoyed the challenge of playing against taller and bigger players. With my tremendous will to win and ability to make plays for my team, I could easily outrun and out jump most of them.

In the seventh game of that season, we played against our long-time traditional rival school, the C.K. McClatchy Lions. It was ironic because McClatchy High is where I would have gone if we had not moved away from Land Park. But now we lived in Oak Park, I was a Dragon, and they were the enemy.

To make this contest even hotter, the coach who had cut me from the flag football team a year ago, when I was in the ninth grade at Peter Lassen Junior High, was now the head JV coach at McClatchy. Because he had cut me, I was extremely motivated to play against McClatchy. I could barely wait to show this coach what kind of player I was. Needless to say, I had the best game of my sophomore season. I was all over that field, covering their receivers, knocking down balls, and making tackles. Each time I made a good play, I ran over to the McClatchy bench to taunt their coach, saying things like, "Too small to play, huh!", "This is what too small looks like!", "You had the opportunity to coach this, but you couldn't see this!", and "I bet you wish you had me now!" I tormented that coach all game long and the Sac High Dragons ended up beating the McClatchy Lions forty-four to zero.

I enjoyed a wonderful athletic career in high school because I was surrounded by a team of hungry, hard-working, and talented athletes who wanted to use their athletic ability to earn a college scholarship and become the next great success story in our neighborhood. In 1972, we won the CIF State Meet in track and field, and the next year, in 1973, we were number one in the Sacramento Metro League football rankings and ended up going undefeated in league play. We ended the year eleven, one, and one.

In 1973, the summer before my senior year, I knew I'd be the starting strong side cornerback, but as a senior, I wanted to go out with a bang and do something special in my final season. So, I secretly decided to try being a two-way starter and play both offense and defense. This meant that I would also tryout to play halfback as well as defensive back. Playing the halfback position at Sac High would allow me to play a big role in the offensive scheme for the Dragons, which in turn would give me the opportunity to be seen by many colleges.

Things were looking up and I was excited about the possibilities of the approaching football season. Yet, the question being rehearsed over and over in my mind was, is football where I'm going to do something special, make a name for myself, and establish a legacy? I was searching for purpose, significance, and legacy, and that is why I secretly began to train for both starting positions, starting halfback and starting strong cornerback, for the Sac High Dragons. Every day after regular practice with the team, I went home, ate dinner, rested for a little while, and then went to the park to train another hour and a half by myself.

That summer, Coach Hotel sent me to a week-long football camp at Southern Oregon College in Ashland, Oregon. I was put on a bus with several other athletes from the Sacramento and Stockton areas to attend. It was on this trip that I saw snow for the very first time. Little did I know that this trip would change my life forever.

When we arrived at the camp, we were given a packet detailing the schedule along with some inspiring, positive quotes and a Bible. When I was given the Bible, I remember thinking, *Oh no, I am at a Christian camp. I'll be stuck here for a week, away from my family and friends, with all these strange people.* I soon found out this was the Fellowship of Christian Athletes (FCA) Camp, and it was awesome.

FCA Camp turned out to be a really cool experience, and it developed in us a powerful sense of teamwork and togetherness. Because of the highly competitive atmosphere, we quickly became brothers. In between the contests, meals, and workouts, we hung out and talked about real meaningful things, like life, our concerns, our goals, and God.

We were divided up into groups of nine or ten. Our groups were called huddles. During the day, the huddles competed against each other in a series of contests in a quest to be crowned Camp Champions.

Each huddle had a huddle leader, and my leader was a guy named Jeff Seiman. Jeff was a professional football player, the starting middle linebacker for the Minnesota Vikings. I had seen him play on TV and was thrilled to be in his huddle. He was very down to earth, transparent, and kind.

Also at camp was an inspirational fitness training guru named Ben Parks from the San Francisco Bay Area. When I shared with Jeff that I wanted to play college football and possibly pro football, he invited me to train with him and Ben.

While everyone else at FCA Camp started each morning with breakfast at 8:00, Ben had me up at 6:00 a.m. running the steep hills of Ashland, Oregon. Then after that, it was off to the weight room for lifting. Breakfast didn't come until after all of that! Those workouts were grueling, and they hurt really bad. I wanted to quit so many times, but I kept going because I didn't want to appear soft. Mostly though, it was because I didn't want to disappoint Ben or Jeff.

Each night after dinner we had what they called "program." At program, a point status report was given on how the daily huddle contests were going. We also sang songs and listened to a variety of guest speakers.

For program on the second night of camp, the guest speaker was Tom Landry, the legendary head football coach of the Dallas Cowboys. During his presentation, Coach Landry boldly shared the testimony of his relationship with Jesus Christ and what Jesus meant to him as his Lord and Savior. His testimony was so impressive that I gave my life to Jesus Christ and asked him to be my Lord and Savior that night. When I got home from FCA Camp, I was much improved as an athlete, but, more importantly, I had become a much better person. Because of the challenge, encouragement, and affirmations from Ben and Jeff, I came home more intensely committed to attaining my goals. Because I had given my life to Jesus Christ, I had received a new, powerful level of confidence and peace.

When the Sac High football practices began in August, I shocked everyone. I was much stronger, faster, and more intense than I had ever been before, and everyone could see it.

When I told everyone I was going to try out for halfback as well as cornerback, I don't think anyone took me seriously, including the coaches. During training camp, as expected, I won the starting strong-side cornerback position, but for the halfback position, I was sitting in the number three spot on the depth chart. I had one final chance to win the halfback position in a scrimmage game against Washington High School in West Sacramento, which was one week before our first real game.

During this scrimmage game, I started at the strong-side corner and performed well. I knew that I had secured that position. At the halfback position, though, it was much different because I had to sit and wait for the two other running backs to play before I could compete. Fortunately for me, neither one of them played well. They both made several mistakes, so the door was clearly open for me to succeed.

When my opportunity to play came, I took full advantage of it. I only got three plays: the last three plays of the scrimmage game. My first play was a triple-option run right, which involved a fake handoff to the fullback, a pull by the quarterback, and then a pitch to me. When our quarterback, Jim Breech, pitched me the ball, I caught it and hit the gas with all that I had and outran everyone to the end zone for a seventy-five-yard touchdown! The feeling was exhilarating, and I wanted more.

Play number two was the same play called to the left side, and just like my first carry, I ran it all the way into the endzone for another touchdown, this time forty-five yards. The third play was the very same play again, to the right side for another forty-five-yard touchdown! I carried the ball three times, for three touchdowns. Because of that performance, I was given the starting halfback position.

Here again God was at work. At five foot six and a half inches tall and 140 pounds, I was the starting cornerback and the starting running back at one of the powerhouse football schools in the state of California. Even though I had no previous experience at running the ball, I led the nation in rushing average for the first four weeks of my senior year with an average of nearly twelve yards per carry.

For the 1973-1974 football season, we ended up with eight wins and two losses. But the real blessing is that I was able to play on this team with my brother Don. Don was a great wide receiver, and he made playing football lots of fun for me because, of course, we had our own competition going on about who would score the most touchdowns. I think Don eventually won. He ended up getting a scholarship the next year to play football at Weber State University in Ogden, Utah.

That year, in 1973, the Sac High Dragons were very hard to beat because we actually had six sets of brothers on the team: the Thomases, the DeLoaches, the Dillons, the Ketchums, the Robinsons, and the Wares. In fact, this was such a big deal that UPI took a photo of all of us that ended up on many sports pages across the country.

Because our team was loaded with so much speed and talent, I ended up with almost 800 yards rushing and an average of almost six yards per carry. With this level of performance and my 3.95 GPA, I was hoping to get a football scholarship. Several schools were interested, but Boise State was the school that showed up at Sac High to sign me.

I will never forget that day. It was in early February when Boise State came to sign me. I was called out of class to Coach Hotel's office. When I arrived, I saw the Boise State assistant coach, Coach Hotel, Alva Liles, and Seth Sandronsky. Boise had already signed Alva Liles, a six foot three, 255-pound defensive tackle with tremendous speed and power, who would eventually become a three-time All-American for Boise State and later signed by the Washington Redskins. They also had signed Seth Sandronsky. He was a six foot four, 278-pound offensive tackle who moved well and was very light on his feet. Now it was my turn to sign.

As I approached the table, the Boise State assistant coach suddenly said, "Wait! I don't think I can take him. He's kind of small and I just don't think he can make it in our conference." *Wow!* I'm thinking to myself. *Here we go again with this talk of me being too small.*

Coach Hotel asked, "What do you mean? This is the same guy you saw on film. He's small but he's fast, tenacious, and tough, and he's never been injured. He's my team captain, he's responsible, and gets good grades. I can assure you he'll be an asset to your team."

"I'm sorry, coach," the Boise assistant coach replied. "I just don't think I can take him back." I was so mad, hurt, disappointed, and frustrated. I had the grades, the talent, the stats, the film, the desire, the toughness, and the maturity to play college football. But once again, I was being denied because of my size.

The sad thing about this scenario was that I hadn't had my growth spurt yet. My parents had enrolled me in school a year early and, as a result, I was always a bit smaller than most of the boys in my class. The irony was that, before the next football season began, I grew by three and a half inches and thirty-five pounds and was now five feet ten inches tall and 175 pounds.

COACH HOTEL

I'd like to take a moment in my story to acknowledge and honor my high school varsity football Coach, Dave Hotel. He was a very good man. He had a tough exterior and wore it well around most people, probably because he had to as a white man working in Oak Park. But he was really an exceptionally funny, kind and thoughtful man.

During my senior year, I was given the opportunity to be Coach Hotel's office assistant, and I saw how he helped so many people on the Sac High campus. He was always so kind to me. He encouraged and inspired me. He believed in me and helped me develop a larger vision for my life. He knew I didn't have a father in my life and stepped up in many ways. He bought my football cleats, sent me to FCA camp, and tried hard to help me get a football scholarship.

Two years after I left high school, he died of a brain aneurysm while backing up a driver's training vehicle on campus. It really broke my heart because I never had the opportunity to thank him for all the good things he did for me and Don.

DRUMS

I had another passion in high school besides playing football. It was playing the drums, any kind of drums—bongos, congas, timbales, timpani, and a regular drum set. I wanted to learn how to play every style of music: gospel, rock, R&B, funk, jazz, Latin, country, classical, fusion, and swing. After testing high for musical aptitude in second grade at Riverside Elementary School, I was given the opportunity to play an instrument. Even though my father played the keyboards, I always loved the drums. I don't know why, but I always wanted to play the drums.

I remember the first time I saw a set of drums. This old man played them at my grandfather's church in Madera, California. As a young child, the sight of a full set of drums intrigued me and I ran up to the front of the church to watch him play. I guess it was in the blood because, years later, I found out that my grandfather, Lester Robinson I, was a jazz drummer in San Francisco.

My mother knew I loved the drums but had already made up her mind there would not be any of that kind of racket in her house. So, when it came time for me to choose the instrument I would play, she said I could play any instrument I wanted except the drums and that I'd better not come home with a pair of drumsticks. Because I knew I wouldn't be allowed to play the drums, I chose to play the clarinet. I really don't know why I chose it. Maybe it was because my best friend, Tommy Barens, had chosen it.

I ended up playing the clarinet for five years and I was pretty good. I even made the All-City band. One year after my father left us in Oak Park, during my sixth-grade year, I quit playing the clarinet because the school said they didn't have any more. So, I didn't play anything again until the end of the ninth grade.

It all began when my cousin, Andy Flennoy, brought his drum set to church, and I was fascinated again. I went to Skips Music store and bought myself a drum instructional book, a pair of drum sticks just like the ones Andy used, and I began to teach myself to play. I basically learned by watching and copying Andy and any other drummers I would see playing live or on TV. I also played along with record albums. I became a drum fanatic and, within six months, was playing at church during worship and with the Christ Temple Radio Choir. I also played in the marching band and the stage band at Sac High.

My stage band director was David Kahn, who later become one of the top A&Rs in the recording business for Columbia Records and

Warner Bros. Records. Under Mr. Kahn's watchful eye, I quickly learned the skills needed to become a professional drummer. Because I didn't own a drum set, he let me practice in the music room during lunch. Sometimes he would snatch me up in his Volkswagen van and let me play with him and his band at various gigs.

Because I was playing so much, I soon became a quite talented drummer and was being recognized by the music community as a young prodigy. I was invited to attend several colleges and music schools, including the prestigious Berklee College of Music in Boston, Massachusetts. As a teenager, I won several honors at stage band competitions and music festivals. I was soon being approached to play for recording artists like Lou Rawls and The Spinners.

The question in my mind at the time was, *Is playing the drums where I am supposed to make a name and establish a legacy?* The thing that kept me from going on the road to play professionally was that I knew I was a part of some very special and talented sports teams, and I really wanted to play high school football and run track with my friends. I felt that, because I was young and strong, I should focus on sports now because those were qualities you needed to compete in that arena. I felt I could always get back into music because age didn't really matter.

Looking back, I believe God used sports to keep me home and grounded. Only he knows what might have happened if I would have become a professional musician traveling around the world at the tender, vulnerable age of sixteen years old.

CHAPTER 8

PANTHERS AND GATORS

After graduating from Sacramento High School without any college football scholarship offers, I still wanted to play. I had a burning desire to prove that not only was I good, but I could be one of the best. My dream school was the University of Southern California. I wanted more than anything in the world to be a USC Trojan. They were the best of the best. They had the best band, the best cheerleaders, the best mascot, and, most definitely, the best team. I would have done anything for a chance to play for Coach John McKay and line up as the starting tailback at "Tailback U," but it wasn't to be.

That summer (1974), I got a job as a lifeguard for the City of Sacramento, at the pool in Southside Park. Besides that, all summer long, all I did was train for football. I didn't have a car, so I rode my ten-speed bike the seven miles between home and work and back each day as fast and as hard as I could to further train my legs. During my breaks, I lifted weights, ran sprints, and ran pass patterns for whatever quarterbacks I could find to throw passes to me.

Because I still wanted to play football, I had to go to junior college. Sacramento City College (SCC) was the nearest one. At that time, no one wanted to play football at Sac City College, because their football program was terrible. I remember so often thinking this was a big mistake, that I should not be there, that I was better than this and should be playing in a much more superior program. Just the thought of playing at SCC made me angry, but I wanted to continue playing football. In high school, I worked hard to get good grades and had proven on the football field that I could be very competitive at the major college level. But now, because some coach felt that I was too small, I was denied the opportunity.

When I reluctantly showed up at SCC to check in and pick up my football equipment, Paul Baker, a bubbly white man with a thick southern drawl, welcomed me. "What's your name, son? Where are you from? And what position do you play?" Then he said jokingly, "You're kinda small, aren't ya? I don't know if we have anything left that will fit you."

Oh, no he didn't! Why did he say that? I told him my name was Les Robinson, and that I was from Sac High. I then cursed him out and told him they didn't deserve me and that he should be glad I came to his sorry school. He just looked at me and seemed to understand that I felt I shouldn't have to be there. Thankfully, even though we started out on a bad note, Paul Baker and I later became very good friends.

Playing football at SCC was atrocious for me that first year. It was like I was stuck in a terrible nightmare that I couldn't wake myself up from. We lost every single game. Yes, it was hard to believe or even imagine it. I never lost ten games in junior high and high school put together, but in my first year of junior college, we lost all ten. I was embarrassed, frustrated, and ashamed to be a part of such an abysmal program. I wanted to quit, but I didn't know how to.

To make ourselves feel better and get over the pain of consistently losing, my best friend on the team, Frank Crosby, and I would do daily spoofs on the antics of the team in a make-believe sports production we called "The SCC Comedy Hour." Usually after practice, our SCC Comedy Hour presentations cracked jokes about everybody involved with the football program: coaches, players, refs, the fans, and the administration. No one was spared.

Despite the fact that we didn't win, I still got better as a football player because I had to get stronger, faster, and tougher if I wanted to be a successful running back. Our line was so small that, for me to get any positive yardage on plays, I had to make my own hole by either faking the opponents out or running right through them. The lack of good blocking made me become a much more physical, determined, and creative runner.

During my second year at SCC, I was elected by the players and coaches as one of the team captains. Our team wasn't much better that year, but we were able to win four games. Immediately after the season was over, I met with the athletic director and told him how frustrated I was and that I had just wasted two years of eligibility at SCC. I told him that the football program was a joke because no one cared whether we won or lost, especially our head coach. Fortunately for the school, our head coach later resigned and the next year, with a new head coach, SCC won the Junior College Football National Championship.

SAN FRANCISCO STATE

While attending Sacramento City College, I worked after school and managed to save enough money to buy a car. I also had an opportunity to play football at San Jose State University, but if I attended there, I would not be able to purchase a car. So, I chose to attend San Francisco State University instead.

That was a huge mistake. For one, San Jose State had a much better football program, and their games were broadcast on TV, providing the exposure I needed to make the NFL; and two, I discovered very quickly I really didn't need a car because just about everything was within walking distance from campus.

When I checked in for the San Francisco State football program, I was in tip-top football shape. I was five feet ten inches tall and weighed 187 pounds. I could run the forty-yard dash in 4.35 seconds, bench press 405 pounds and squat 635 pounds. I was extremely football fit. Like my halfback experience in high school, I was not considered the starter, but on day one of summer practice, I was ranked in the number seven spot at halfback. My focus now was to earn the starting halfback position.

One of the main challenges of making the San Francisco State team was that it was a veteran-heavy squad, consisting of many returning players with already well-developed relationships and alliances. For example, some of the upperclassmen from specific geographical areas such as Oakland, Compton, San Diego, Stockton, and Sacramento were fighting to make sure their homeboys inherited certain positions. So, not only was I competing with the guys at my position of halfback, but I was also going up against guys on the defensive side of the team who wanted to make me look bad so that their friends could win out. To secure the starting position of halfback, I had only about six weeks to work my way through this gauntlet of obstacles and alliances.

All these games didn't matter much to me, though, because I experienced similar scenarios in high school. Instead, I saw this as my last opportunity to do something great in football, and I was totally committed to that pursuit.

The day I left for San Francisco State, I remember getting into my car to leave my mother, my siblings, and my girlfriend for what I knew would be the last time. I knew I was now on my own and could not come back. Because I had no financial safety net, I absolutely had to be successful there. All my way down the I-80 freeway from Sacramento to San Francisco, I cried because I knew this was it. This time at San Francisco State University would be do or die.

RACE REVELATIONS

When pre-season football camp began, we did "three-a-days," meaning that practice was at three different times every day. Which meant we were on campus from sunrise to sunset. Our longest break between each day's practices was usually around lunchtime, and we would eat, relax, and sometimes swim. I remember the first time I decided to take a swim. I hadn't noticed it, but I was the only African American on the team that swam. The rest of the brothers just walked or played in the water.

During one of those breaks, I casually dove into the pool using a racing dive and swam to the other side of the pool. As I came out of the water, I noticed a group of white guys on the team shouting and screaming because they said they'd been told that blacks can't swim. "That was a lie," they said, "because, man! You swim like a fish!" Little did they know that as a child, I swam competitively, and I was currently a pool manager and water safety instructor for the City of Sacramento.

In training camp a few days later, during lunch, I was eating and two of the white linemen from somewhere in the hills of California came over to me and voiced their concerns that I and my roommate, Frank Crosby, might be unhappy and possibly planning to leave San Francisco State to go play at San Jose State. Some of our players had already left to join the San Jose squad and had asked me to think about it, too. These teammates then told us we were good players, and they didn't want us to go. I thanked them for their compliments and concerns but assured them that I was not unhappy and that I was not leaving San Francisco State.

I asked them why they thought I was sad and possibly leaving. Their response was, "Well, you and Frank don't laugh a lot and talk jive like the other black guys on the team. You know, like Jimmy Walker's character on 'Good Times.'" I could not believe what I had just heard, the thought that all blacks acted like J.J. I told them that blacks in general didn't talk jive and act like Jimmy Walker. I told them that "Good Times" was merely a comedy TV show, and that thousands of African American men and women are doctors, lawyers, college professors, inventors, and businessmen. They said they had never met anyone black and that their only exposure to blacks before coming to San Francisco State was what they saw on TV.

It was hard to believe the perceptions that other Americans had about African Americans in 1977. These two experiences at San Francisco State were proof that most cities and communities in America were still segregated, even in progressive California.

During that pre-season football camp, I demonstrated to my teammates and coaches that I should be the number one halfback. But the upperclassmen were working hard to freeze me out of the action and keep me from getting plays. I finally broke through just like I did in high school during that final scrimmage game. This time, I had lots of solid runs and caught several passes, which showed that I was a very skilled and versatile halfback. But the real deciding play happened near the end of the scrimmage.

The play was a double-down kick out power run to the right. I was given the ball and darted towards the hole designed to break right inside the right tackle's outside hip. I turned up into the hole and was immediately hit by the middle linebacker head up. I accelerated into him with all my might, hit him and spun outside, and was hit again by the outside linebacker. I spun again, off his tackle inside, and headed up-field. There, I was met by the strong safety and the left corner together. I accelerated hard and low, dipping down low to split them, and then sprinted toward the goal line to score a sixty-yard touchdown.

While attending San Francisco State, I developed a mean, dark side of me because I felt like I had to be extremely hard to survive in this crazy dog-eat-dog environment. I saw displayed daily what I would call the ugliness of life: ruthless, selfish behavior, and a total lack of respect for people, property, and relationships. In the Bay Area, it seemed as though nothing was sacred. All I saw was pride, greed, lust, and selfishness. It was a dark time.

I was nineteen years old when my father finally saw me play football. It was during my junior year at San Francisco State, and we were playing in our first televised game there in a long time. It was broadcasted nationally, in fact, with popular singer and San Francisco State alumnus Johnny Mathis singing the National Anthem. So, this was a big, big game for us. Our opponent was the powerful Division One Double A University of Nevada Reno Wolf Pack. During the week prior to the game, the *San Francisco Chronicle* published a picture of me along with an article about the upcoming contest on the front page of the sports section. My father worked in downtown San Francisco managing a large team for the State of California Department of

Highways and Bridges. One of his employees saw my picture and showed it to him, asking if there was any relation.

That was how my father found out I was an athlete and living in San Francisco. He showed up to the game and enjoyed himself. My girlfriend told me it made him proud to see me play. Little did he know that I was even happier than him because it gave me an opportunity to show him a side of me he never knew existed.

We ended up losing to the University of Reno that day. I had a pretty good game but, because we lost, it didn't mean much. I don't know why, but even though my father enjoyed himself, he never came to see me play again.

BERKELEY

During my time at San Francisco State, we had a racist coach on staff who had been involved in quite a few confrontations with many of the African Americans on the team because of the condescending way he spoke to us. He didn't respect or like us, and we all knew it. He even tried to get physical with some of us. One time during a game, he tried to grab me by the shoulder pads like I was a boy. I immediately knocked his hands down and told him that if he ever tried to put his hands on me again, I would break him up. He didn't like it because I was confident in myself and my ability to play football. He told me to my face that he was going to recruit another running back who could beat me so that he could get me out of the starting lineup. I took it as a personal challenge and told him to go for it.

When I showed up for the first football practice of my senior year, sure enough, three new white running backs were all brought there to beat me. It didn't matter one bit to me because I always prepared each off season to be the starting halfback no matter where I was or who showed up. This plan of his turned out to be a total waste of time. These new halfbacks he brought in didn't challenge me in any phase of the game, and I clearly beat them out for the starting halfback position.

That didn't matter at all, however, because this coach had decided that regardless of how well I performed, he was going to play one of these running backs ahead of me. It was very upsetting because not only did I know but the whole team knew what was going on.

Our first home game that year was played on Saturday, September 17th, against Cal Poly Pomona at 1:00 p.m. Unbeknownst to our coaching staff, our team had been invited to a huge party happening the night before by University of California, Berkeley, at a large hotel in Berkeley. Because I was angry that this racist coach had told me I would not be in the starting lineup the next day, I decided to go check this party out.

When we arrived, the place was jumping! It was packed with beautiful people and alive with excitement. Hundreds showed up dressed to the max, ready to party hardy with whistles, tambourines, and shakers. People were dancing, laughing, drinking, and smoking a lot of pot. Some of them were literally dancing out of their clothes. The place was hot and weed was being passed all around the room.

Because I knew I wasn't going to play the next day, I decided to smoke some weed, too. So, I got high. I mean super high. I was what you would call blind. I was so high when we left the party sometime after 3:00 a.m. that I still don't remember how I got home. When I woke up a few hours later that morning, I was still high. So, I took a nice, long, hot shower hoping it would bring me down. But it didn't.

Our pre-game activities typically began with breakfast at 8:00 a.m. and then we would hang out for a while before going to team meetings that started around 11:00 a.m. During this breakfast, I ate a ton of food and drank lots of hot coffee, but that didn't help me come down at all. I was really starting to get worried now because during team meetings, we would have to answer offensive questions concerning specific situations and calls relative to the game, and I was in no condition to do that.

It was about that time that I told my teammate, Frank Crosby, who was our starting wide receiver, about my dilemma. He advised me to hurry back to the dorms and take another quick, hot shower. I ran home and took another hot shower, but I was still high. Because I couldn't come down, I began to wonder if I smoked some weed that was laced with PCP, or "Angel Dust."

Even though the racist coach told me I wouldn't be playing, I knew I would be called on anyway, because the guy he chose to start was weak and afraid. I knew it would only be a matter of time before all the coaching staff got tired of the tiptoeing and call me into the game. But what worried me most was that I had never done anything high, especially play football.

Football for a running back is serious business. The position demands high levels of contact, most of which is at a high velocity of speed. Because of the physical demands of the halfback position, I knew I could get seriously hurt, or even paralyzed, if I wasn't mentally right.

At 11:20 a.m., we were instructed to get dressed, and I was still high as a kite. At 11:45 a.m., the specialist or special team players were called out to the field to begin warmups, and I was still high. At 12:10 p.m., we began team warmups, and I was still high. I was hoping no one could tell, especially the coaches.

At 1:00 p.m., the game started. I had some sense of relief because we lost the coin toss and had to kick the ball to the opposing team. Had we won the coin toss and the opportunity to receive the opening kickoff, I would have been in the game and on the field high, waiting to return the kick.

I stood on the sidelines watching the game for about a quarter and a half before the coaching staff got tired of the ineffectiveness of the halfback the racist coach tried to replace me with. I was called off the sidelines and sent into the game high for a play that was called to me. I was tripping hard because I was unfamiliar with how to handle being this intoxicated, and now I was being called on by my team to make a play.

The play called was a forty-eight toss sweep right. The quarterback pitched the ball to me going right. I accelerated hard to the outside, I sharply cut back inside, and then I broke back outside hard and hit the gas up the sideline for a forty-eight-yard touchdown. It was crazy because when I sped through the end zone and looked up into the crowd, everyone seemed to be jumping up and down in slow motion. I played the rest of the game and after a fierce battle we beat Cal Poly Pomona twenty-one to eighteen.

After the game, I was able to come down from my high. I thanked God for His mercy and grace and for protecting me from my own foolishness. That day, I promised God and myself that I would never do anything like that again, and I didn't.

SUICIDE?

Later that semester, after football season was over, I was very stressed out and worrying a lot. I had run out of money, I was almost out of food, and I was suffering from depression. One night, I received a phone call from my girlfriend in Sacramento and it wasn't a good one, which made things even worse. I wanted to go home to resolve the situation, but I didn't even have money for gas. I was desperate, so I called my father to see if he would lend me some money, but he said he didn't have any. That conversation only sent me deeper into depression. To escape the pain and frustration, I decided I would get some weed from some of the guys in the dorms and get high. They were more than happy to give me five or six joints.

Verducci Hall was the dorm I stayed in at San Francisco State. It was the dorm everyone wanted to live in back in the day. The front side overlooked beautiful Lake Merced, and the back overlooked the football and baseball practice fields. Verducci Hall was the newest and most expensive of the San Francisco State University dorms. It was also the tallest of the dorms at fifteen stories high. I lived on the seventh floor, which was known at that time as the party floor.

That night, my roommate had already gone home for the weekend. I was alone, hurting, hungry, broke, and depressed. I felt like now that football season was over, no one really cared about me, so I smoked the weed. All of it.

Suddenly, I began to think I didn't want to be here. I didn't want to deal with this pain and frustration any longer. I was tired of it all. *What's the use?*, I thought to myself. *I can just end it now by going out on my balcony and jumping.* I wasn't afraid of death or pain. I had just weeks earlier witnessed a student jump off the balcony from the fifteenth floor and die. I thought I could just do this now and it all would be over. I knew it would happen quickly.

In a moment of anguish, I stepped out onto my balcony preparing to jump. I was out there for about half an hour contemplating the outcome of what I was about to do. The one thing that stopped me from jumping was the thought that I would end up in Hell, and I did not want that. Eventually, I went back into my room, laid across my bed, and cried myself to sleep.

The devil tried to convince me to take my own life in a moment of intense depression and loneliness. Looking back at this very dark moment in my life, I am so glad I didn't commit suicide because I had so much to live for and I would have missed out on all of it because of some relatively petty, temporary feelings.

As I grew older and experienced more of life, I learned that thoughts of suicide happen in a great number of the world's population. Suicide has been one of the most deceptive tricks of the enemy to take out God's dear children. It is the second leading cause of death in Americans between the ages of ten to thirty-four years. The facts are that annually, twelve million Americans seriously think about taking their own lives. If you are having thoughts of suicide, don't think that you are weird or alone. Please reach out for help. There are many people, but most of all God, who value, love, and care about you. Please contact the Suicide and Crisis lifeline by calling or texting the three-digit number 988 or log on to 988lifeline.org.

VIC ROWEN

Vic Rowen was a great coach, not just because he was a great game strategist, but because he was a real leader of men. He taught and believed in good values and principles, such as promptness, integrity, and hard work. But most of all, he cared about his players, not just for how we played but he also cared about the way we lived and the choices we made in life.

After I played my last game of football at San Francisco State, Coach Vic called me into his office and told me he knew how strongly I wanted to play in the National Football League. His words to me were, "Lester, I know you want to play in the league, and you can play in the league, but I am not for you playing in the league. I shouldn't say this to you of all people, because I know that it will only motivate you to want it more, but Lester, they will just beat you up. Yes, you'll have some fun and do good. But, in the end, you'll just be broken, and they won't care." He went on to say, "You have a good mind and are a good student. You don't need football. Football needs you. They will just use you up and spit you out."

Of course, I didn't want to hear any of that. I was young, strong, and willing to sacrifice myself to the football gods in search of fame, fortune, and a legacy. For many years after that conversation, I was angry at God and Coach Rowen because I wanted so badly to play in the NFL so that I could prove to myself and others that I was one of the best running backs ever.

When I reflect and think about what Coach Rowen said and how adamant he was about me not playing, I know that he loved and cared about me. I feel that he knew, or at least had some concerns, that many young men's lives were being compromised because of the effects of repeated high velocity hits and the traumatic brain injuries that resulted.

Coach Rowen's insights and wise words saved my life, and I thank God he did. Coach Vic Rowen died on January 14, 2013, at ninety-three years old. He turned San Francisco State University into a premier small college football powerhouse. NFL Super Bowl-winning coaches Mike Holmgren with the Green Bay Packers, Andy Reid with the Philadelphia Eagles and Kansas City Chiefs, and Bob Toledo of UCLA and Tulane, were some of the coaches he mentored.

Once again, because of my relationship with Coach Vic Rowen, God had protected me and saved me for something much more important than football.

THE LEGACY OF DANIEL BLUE

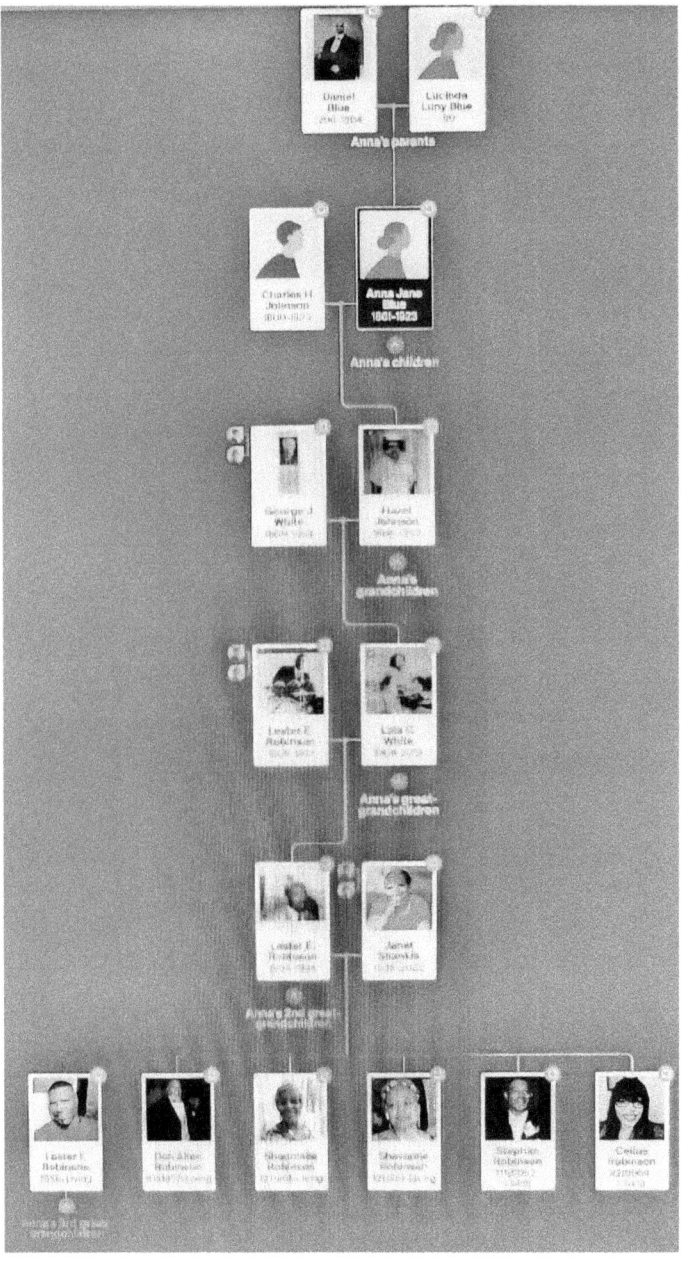

Daniel Blue's Ancestry Family Chart

Daniel Blue

St. Andrews AME Church 1867

St. Andrew AME Church—Present day

Gen. John A. Sutter

The original court records of Daniel Blue's petition to free Edith from enslavement are located at the Center for Sacramento History. *(Asal*

Official Governor Portrait of Peter Hardeman Burnett
Credit: Peter H. Burnett, California's First Governor - Pacific Bank:

Great Grandmother,
Hazel Johnson White

Grandmother, Lola White
Robinson-Reed

Lester Robinson, Jr.—Les's father

Mother Janet Robinson, sons, Les and Don

Lester & Don Robinson

Grandma Hazel, Brothers Don & Les Robinson

Les at 4 years old

Les at 17 years old

Les at SFSU

District Elder Robert B. Holman, Sr.
(Les' mentor)

Les Robinson's Twin sisters, Shaunielle and Shevonne

Family photo: Les, Shaunielle, Don, Shevonne, Celine, Mother, Janet, Stephan

Les Robinson

Les Robinson, center, the great-great-great grandson of St. Andrews AME founding pastor Daniel Blue, speaks during the church's 172 anniversary celebration. **Antonio R. Harvey, OBSERVER**

Don Robinson, Lester Robinson, Johnny Ware, Sr.

The day of the interview with NBC News

CHAPTER 9

"HELL NO!"

During my college football days at San Francisco State University from 1976 to 1977, I was so obsessed with football and trying to position myself to make the NFL that little else mattered. I indeed became a true football junkie or rather, even worse, a football zombie. All I wanted to do was get bigger, stronger, faster, and smarter so that I could live out my dream of playing in the NFL.

I studied and focused on football day and night. I ate for football. I daydreamed about football. I lived for football. Everything I did was about football. I had little time for anything else except for my girlfriend and then more football. Football had become my idol, and nothing else in the world mattered much to me. Including a relationship with the Lord.

I remember an evening that clearly illustrates this. Late one Sunday night, on October 31st, Halloween of all days, I was returning to San Francisco State from a weekend visit to Sacramento. I remember this because it was daylight saving time when we had to turn the clocks back an hour. This made me very happy because it meant an extra hour for me to spend with my girlfriend on Sunday night.

However, on this Halloween night, the weather was terrible. It was raining cats and dogs, and the wind was blowing with gusts of up to forty to sixty miles per hour. The weather was so bad that I delayed my departure, hoping that it would clear up, but it didn't. On any other Sunday night, I would have just stayed in Sacramento and returned to San Francisco the next morning, but I was scheduled to take a very important exam Monday morning, and I could not miss it.

At about 2:30 in the morning, I decided I needed to leave regardless of the weather. So, I headed down the I-80 freeway, making my way toward San Francisco in my tiny, forest green, 1973 Mercury Capri. I passed through the cities of Vacaville, Fairfield, and Vallejo, crossed the Carquinez Bridge, and fought the wind and rain all the way through Pinole, Richmond, Berkeley, and Emeryville. As I approached the San Francisco /Oakland Bay Bridge, I became eerily aware that I was the only one out here on the freeway in this crazy storm, and it was getting worse!

As I pulled away from the toll booths on the Oakland side of the Bay Bridge, it began to rain so hard that I could barely see, causing me to slow down to about twenty-five miles per hour. During the upward climb on the ramp of the Bay Bridge, I noticed that the bridge was swaying. But did I stop or turn around? No! I foolishly keep going.

At that moment, in the middle of this terrible storm, I heard the voice of the Lord call out to me, "I want you to preach My Word."

Anyone else I think would have been scared. But not me! I wasn't scared. I got mad! I heard the voice of God, and I knew exactly what He wanted. I had heard Him speak to me before, but I didn't want to hear from Him right now. And I especially did not want to hear about me preaching! Because right now, all I wanted to do was finish my college football career, make an NFL team, set myself up financially, retire after five years, and marry my girl.

That was my master plan. That's what I wanted first and foremost. I had already made up my mind that, after I accomplished my own personal goals, then I would surrender my life to God and do anything and everything He wanted me to do.

I just wanted this little span of time to do me; to live my dreams and do whatever I wanted to do. After all, I'd never been able to do what I wanted. As the oldest child in my family, it seemed I was always being put in some position of responsibility to care and look out for somebody else. I just wanted to do something for me for once. I had decided this was going to be my time, and dagnabbit, football was what I was going to do first!

A little bit further on the Bay Bridge, about halfway through its span, I heard God's voice audibly again. "I want you to preach My Word." But this time, I exploded in anger. I rolled down the driver's side window and, in all that wind and rain, I yelled out with all my might, "Hell no!" After I made it to the other side of the Bay Bridge entering San Francisco, the storm suddenly stopped. It was as if God said, "Alright, have it your way!"

Looking back on my life, it's hard to believe I said those things to God, but I did. How could I have been so disrespectful, so irreverent, to the God of heaven and earth, the Master of the universe, the Lord God, who had blessed, protected, and provided for me all my life? How selfish and immature I was. To this day, I am extremely embarrassed and regret the way I initially responded to His will for my life. I should have felt extremely honored that the Lord of Lords and King of Kings had invited me to be a part of His great team of witnesses. Unfortunately, at that time in my life, I was so blind by the agenda of "me" that my pride and selfishness totally hindered my ability to hear God and think with any measure of soundness.

My football career at San Francisco State wasn't exactly what I wanted it to be, but it wasn't bad. I had a few decent games and was able to draw the attention of several NFL teams mainly because, for one, I played for Coach Vic Rowen, who had a tremendous reputation in the NFL for producing very good skill position players at the Division 3 level; and two, I was very strong, very explosive, and had great speed.

REGGIE WHITE

A few years later, God would bring onto the football scene a man, a vessel, who would boldly proclaim the Lord's Gospel message. His name was Reggie White.

Reggie White was a six foot five, 300-pound All-American football player from the University of Tennessee, blessed with tremendous speed and strength. While at Tennessee, he became involved with the Fellowship of Christian Athletes (FCA) and expressed an interest in becoming an evangelist. Soon after, he was ordained as a Baptist minister and acquired the very fitting nickname of "Minister of Defense."

I loved watching Reggie White play. He was a dominant, freakish player who could literally take over a game from the defensive end position. He played in the USFL two years with the Memphis Showboats; and then he played fifteen years in the NFL, eight with the Philadelphia Eagles, six with the Green Bay Packers, and one with the Carolina Panthers. He became one of the most awarded football players of all time, amassing all kinds of records and honors, including:

- First Team All-USFL
- Bart Starr Award
- Super Bowl Champion XXXl
- Two-time NFL Player of the Year
- Three-time NFC Defensive Player of the Year

- Eight-time First Team All-Pro
- Five-time Second Team All-Pro
- Thirteen-time Pro Bowl Selection
- Two-time NFL Sacks Leader
- NFL 100 Sacks Club
- 198 Sacks
- NFL 1980s All-Decade Team
- NFL 75th Anniversary All-Time Team
- NFL 100th Anniversary All-Time Team
- College Football Hall of Fame
- Philadelphia Eagles Hall of Fame
- Pro Football Hall of Fame

Anyone who understands the game of football knows just how remarkable all these honors truly are. But what impressed me even more was that Reggie was a real, ardent witness for Jesus Christ. I loved how boldly he shared his testimony and faith in God in his post-game interviews on Sunday afternoons. He was not ashamed or timid about using the platform of football to share the glorious gospel of Jesus Christ with the world.

For years, while I proudly watched him publicly proclaim his faith in God, at the same time I felt a measure of conviction, wondering if that is how God might have used me had I said yes instead of "Hell no!"

On December 26, 2004, four years after retiring from professional football, Reggie White died from cardiac arrhythmia.

"Hell No!"

When I saw the news reports, I was in utter disbelief. I wept like a baby because I knew that God had called home one of His great warriors. I also knew that Reggie's powerful testimony and witness would be missed. I found solace in the hope that I'll see him again in heaven.

CHAPTER 10

AFTER SFSU

Although Coach Vic Rowen advised me not to pursue a career in the National Football League, I pursued it anyway because, at that time, I felt that football was where God was calling me to do something great and significant with my life. So, at San Francisco State University, I continued to attend classes, workout for possible tryouts, and work at night.

I found a job at SFO, the San Francisco International Airport, loading freight for a small air freight company called Trans West Air Express. My job was to load and weigh pallets of freight and then load them by forklift onto DC 3 airplanes, from 11:00 p.m. to 3:00 a.m. The job was very exhausting because, along with the drive to and from SFO, it required a lot of physical as well as mental energy.

To make matters worse, late in the school year, I had run out of script to purchase food in the dorm cafeteria and was basically living on peanut butter and jelly sandwiches and milk. Between school and a work schedule that allowed me only four hours of rest, plus also trying to maintain my intense physical training regimen on limited food, I was running myself into the ground. I soon got sick and had to go home to Sacramento where I spent a few days in the hospital, diagnosed with what doctors said was fatigue.

While lying there in the hospital, I decided not to return to San Francisco State to finish my last year of school. I decided to take a year off, get a job, and concentrate on my goal of playing football in the NFL, then after that go back to San Francisco State and complete my B.S. degree in physical education. This would allow me to be home near my family and girlfriend while I pursued my dream.

Within a few weeks, I got a job at United Parcel Service (UPS) loading and sorting freight on the night shift from 10:00 pm to 4:00 am. UPS paid very well, so I was able to purchase a new car and rent a nice apartment while I continued to train for an opportunity to play professional football.

One of the tryouts I participated in was for the British Columbia Lions, a Canadian League Football Team. The tryout was a two-day event held on a Saturday and Sunday at Orange Coast College in Costa Mesa, Orange County, California. My girlfriend drove down with me. We arrived in neighboring Huntington Beach early Friday morning, prior to the tryout to get a hotel room and familiarize ourselves with the surrounding area.

We drove to three different hotels in Huntington Beach and all three said, without hesitation, that they were full. After the third rejection we sat in the car and remembered that we were in Orange County, California. We then decided to go back to the first hotel and let my girlfriend go in to book a room. She was a very beautiful and intelligent young lady with light skin and long, pretty hair. It worked. She was able to secure a room in the hotel that was supposedly full because she was beautiful and could pass for white.

Wow! Here we were in 1978, and racial discrimination was alive and well in Huntington Beach, California. It made me so angry that I got an upset stomach and spent a good part of that evening trying to overcome it.

When I showed up for camp the next morning, more than 400 athletes were there to try out for the BC Lions.

The first day of camp went very well for me. I ran a 4.35 in the forty-yard dash on the natural grass field at Orange Coast College. I posted very quick times and made some nice cuts during the movement and agility drills they ran us through. During the actual performance sessions, I didn't drop one pitch, pass, punt, or kick all day.

When I arrived on the second day of tryouts less than one hundred athletes had survived, and as the day went on, more athletes were being released. I was able to put together another great day of work, and at the end of the day there were only two athletes left. Both of us were specialists: a punter, and me returning punts.

At the end of the tryouts, the BC coaches congratulated me and said they were impressed by my level of speed and skill. They said they felt I would be a great asset to their team and hoped they could work things out. They needed to return to Canada, share and discuss the film of the tryouts with the rest of the staff, and check their quota status. They explained to me that in the Canadian Football League, each team was allowed to have a certain percentage of players from the United States based on the number of Canadian players each team had on their rosters. They reconfirmed my contact information and told me they'd call me within a week.

I never heard back from the BC Lions, which left me very disappointed.

The following football season, to keep my skills up, I played on a local minor league professional team with my brother Don. The Sacramento Buffaloes was a good team, made up of a lot of Sacramento area football all-star type players. We were paid weekly and had a nice training staff that included physical therapists, chiropractors, and masseuses. On Tuesday or Wednesday evenings, we were asked to sign autographs at dinners and big parties to help promote the team and bolster attendance at the games. We won most of our games that season and ended up being the California State Champions.

It was a cool experience, and we had lots of fun, but it was not the NFL. I really wanted to play NFL ball, but as time rolled on, it was becoming clear that I would not be getting the opportunities I wanted. I had a nice car, a good job, and my apartment, and I was really sensing the need to get on with life apart from professional football. So, I started attending church religiously, with a focus on developing a more intimate relationship with Jesus Christ.

I began to read and study the Bible voraciously. I couldn't get enough of God's Word or learn enough about Him. I just wanted to know more and more about God and the great love story between Him and His creation. As a result of this growing relationship with Him, I significantly increased my church participation at Christ Temple Apostolic Church. Soon, I was teaching adult Sunday school and began serving on the church's board of directors and as the vice chairman of the men's ministry, "The Brotherhood."

PSALMS 81:10

Christ Temple Apostolic Church was part of the Pentecostal Assemblies of the World organization, or PAW. Our church was known throughout PAW as the church that specialized in the ministry of God's Word, the ministry of music, and the practice of discipling believers.

The winning of non-believers to Christ and their discipling was a constant practice at Christ Temple. The music ministry under the direction of Robert B. Holman Jr. was excellent in terms of presentation and anointing, with the Christ Temple Apostolic Church Choir receiving invitations to sing all over the United States. They were one of the top choirs in the country and by the time I was fifteen years old, they had already released two albums.

But at Christ Temple Apostolic Church, the anointed ministry of God's Word was number one. Our pastor, Elder Robert B. Holman Sr., not only taught us the Word of God in its entirety, but he also expected us to know it and live it daily. He wanted all the ministry staff to be very accurate and excellent in delivery of God's Word. He wanted us to have the anointing of the Holy Spirit on our preaching, so it was very important to him that we possessed and maintained a very real, personal, and intimate relationship with Jesus Christ.

We received from Elder Holman a lot of valuable ministry instruction from the New Testament books of First and Second Timothy, and Titus. These books were actual letters that the Apostle Paul wrote to educate, instruct, and encourage his young pastors, Timothy and Titus, in their teaching of the Christian faith in Asia Minor.

One of Elder Holman's favorite verses was 2 Timothy 4:2, which says, "Preach the word; be instant in season, out of season; reprove, rebuke, exhort with all longsuffering and doctrine" (KJV). From this scripture, he created an exercise he called "Preachers on the Loose." How it worked was that, during any given Friday or Sunday evening service, he would randomly call ministers out of the audience without any prior notification to deliver a five- to ten-minute sermon. These short sermons are very difficult because you must introduce the text, exegete it, and summarize it all in a short period of time. It was tough training, but it kept us studying, praying, and well prepared.

Because of the time, prayer, and training he invested in us, Elder Holman was able to produce many well-seasoned pastors, preachers, and teachers, myself included. In his honor, I will name some of them:

- Bishop David Foster, Sacramento, California
- Bishop Donald R. Black, Alexandria, Virginia
- Bishop Parnell Lovelace, Sacramento, California
- Rabbi Robert B. Holman Jr., Sacramento, California
- Pastor Major Terry, Yuba City, California
- Pastor Arthur Robinson, Modesto, California
- Pastor John Hammond, Maui, Hawaii
- Dr. Carolyn O'Neil, Sacramento, California
- Pastor Charles Warner, Sacramento, California
- Pastor Allen Myrick, Sacramento, California
- Pastor Neil Miller, Sacramento, California
- Pastor Otis Moore, Sacramento, California
- Dr. Zena Randolph, Nolanville, Texas
- Dr. Rhonda Carroll, China
- Pastor Robbie Robinson, Dallas, Texas

In 1981, at the age of twenty-three, I delivered my first major sermon on a Sunday morning live radio broadcast. I was the vice president of our men's ministry at that time and it was fourth Sunday, which at Christ Temple Apostolic Church was "Brotherhood Day." This was the day that the men of the church were responsible to handle all aspects of the service. On Brotherhood Day, the men taught the Sunday school classes, led praise and worship, collected the offerings, served communion, performed the baptisms, and preached the sermons.

I went to church that morning ready to assist our Brotherhood president, Henry Duncan, with running the Sunday worship service. That's when he informs me that everything was covered except that our guest speaker had an emergency and couldn't come. Then Henry looked at me, said, "I heard that you were called to preach. Okay, we'll just let you take his place," and then walked away.

I suddenly felt like the weight of the world had just landed on my shoulders. I had been asked to preach, live on the radio, with no preparation. I immediately went to our green room in the back of the church to pray and ponder what God might have me to say to His people. I was nervous and stressing out when our pastor's wife, Mother Holman, entered the room, put her arms around me, and said, "Son, don't worry. God has got this, and He's given it to you. The Word is already in you. You just need to relax and let Him have His way."

Mother Holman then offered to share a scripture with me. She opened her Bible and read to me Psalms 81:10, which says, "I am the Lord thy God, which brought thee out of the land of Egypt: open thy mouth wide, and I will fill it."

Immediately, a calm peacefulness came over me and a sermon quickly filled my heart. That morning, God blessed me to teach a wonderful sermon from Act 3:1-9, where Peter heals the lame man at the gate called Beautiful. The title of the sermon was "What Do You Have?" It centered around the fact that there is power in the name of Jesus and that we have been given authority to use His name to petition God for the things we need.

God tremendously blessed His Word, the people, and me that Sunday morning. I will never forget the kindness and sensitivity of Mother Holman and the way God used her to give me freedom in the pulpit. Because of her wisdom and council, I have always been free of anxiety when ministering the Word of God.

To this day, I continue to read and meditate on Psalms 81:10 before I speak, and I have shared the comfort of those anointed words with others.

In time, I became a licensed minister in the PAW organization. Not long after that, I was included in the regular speaking rotation for the Sunday morning services at Christ Temple.

In 1978, I proposed to my girlfriend and we were married at Christ Temple Apostolic Church on July 28, 1979. God truly blessed us. We both had great jobs and nice cars, and we lived in a very nice apartment. After a few years, we were blessed to have our first child, a beautiful son named Brandon. Not too long after he was born, we were able to purchase our first home. It was such an awesome and exciting time for us. Everything was coming together very nicely. I had a good job with FedEx, a beautiful wife, a beautiful son, and a brand-new house.

About this same time, I began to learn to play a new instrument, the electric bass guitar. Through the years, I had sung the bass part in choirs, and as a drummer, I had developed an ear to clearly hear the bass line, so the transition to the bass guitar was easy. Soon, I began to write, play, and record contemporary Gospel music. I started hanging out in the recording studio with a friend of mine, Robert Brookins, who was a phenomenal musician, singer, and songwriter who had already played with artists like George Duke, Stanley Clarke, Stephanie Mills, George Howard, and Earth, Wind & Fire.

Another great musician, singer, and songwriter that I had the privilege to learn from was Brian Alexander Morgan, the composer and writer of the music for the popular R&B group, SWV (Sisters with Voices). Brian let me hang out and watch him create and mix track after track after track.

These fantastic musical artists inspired me to create my own, unique style of music, as well. I soon assembled a hybrid contemporary gospel group called "Ekklesia." It was made up of a blend of secular musicians and gospel singers. Because of our instrumentation and sound, we were quite controversial in the church world because we were presenting the gospel of Jesus Christ but in a real funky, non-traditional way.

According to most of the Pentecostal churches, we sounded "worldly," which meant we sounded like secular bands. It was a style the Pentecostal church was not accustomed to embracing. But that didn't really bother me much because I felt God was calling us to do something different and revolutionary. If we were going to get the attention of the world and, in particular, people who didn't know Christ, we had to present the gospel in a manner that would get their attention. I believed that, through this new evangelical concept and style of music, God would enable us to influence thousands. This was another area where I felt I would find significance and leave a legacy that would last beyond me.

I quickly became one of the top bassists in the Sacramento area and was being asked to play for many touring gospel recording artists, including Richard Smallwood, The Clark Sisters, Vickie Winans, Shirley Ceasar, and Vanessa Bell Armstrong. In no time at all, things began to really pick up and word was spreading fast about Ekklesia, the gospel group with today's sound. We were working very hard, writing our own original songs, and going into the recording studio to send our music out to people in the music industry. Sylvia Rhone of Epic Records and Sony Music Entertainment was one of the people who began showing interest. It was a very exciting time.

DIVORCE?

Everything was going great. My wife and I had just had a second child, a beautiful daughter we named Danielle. We were also able to purchase our second house, in which I planned to build our own private recording studio. I was on my way to having it all and doing it all. Little did I know it would all soon come to an end.

After about two months of living in our new home, my wife informed me she was not happy in our marriage. She said she wanted a different lifestyle and asked for a divorce. Our marriage wasn't perfect. We had our problems and needed to work on some things, but I never felt divorce was the appropriate solution.

I was extremely disappointed, embarrassed, and hurt. It seemed as if my whole world had come to an abrupt stop. Once again, a plan I thought would be perfect actually ended, but this time I was caught totally off guard and had no plan for recovery. This was not what I wanted. This is not the life I had planned, envisioned, or hoped for. This was not the kind of legacy I wanted to leave for my children. How could God get glory and be honored in this?

As a husband, father, and leader, I felt like a total failure. This was the one thing I never wanted. I knew very well the specter of being raised without a father, and I didn't want my children to have that experience. I also knew first-hand that no one wins in divorce. Everyone gets hurt and some people never recover. I kept asking within myself, where was God? And how could He allow this to happen to me?

I was so angry and demoralized. My plans, hopes, and dreams, everything I had worked so hard for—my wife, our family, our house, my reputation, and my gospel music career—was now going up in smoke. I totally lost the desire to play music. I stopped practicing, writing, and recording. I broke up the group and went into a shell.

I was alone, confused, and ashamed. In the Sacramento area, I was a well-known athlete, musician, and preacher. At this point, all I wanted to do was hide, but there was no place to hide. The situation seemed totally hopeless, and I became incredibly frustrated. I was angry at the situation. I was angry at my wife. I was angry at myself. But most of all, I was angry at God.

For the first time in my life, I didn't give a rip about anybody or anything. This mindset was totally out of character for me. I had very quickly morphed into a person I didn't know or even want to be. I had become a very dangerous, ticking time bomb to the point that I started taking my loaded nine-millimeter pistol with me everywhere I went.

I quit reading and studying the Bible. I quit praying. I quit going to church. I didn't want to hear about God or His love, His promises, the church, or anything related to the Christian faith.

My life was in complete shambles. My heart was in the state of utter chaos. I felt I had totally surrendered everything to God, but He did nothing to help me in my time of need. I thought He was going to let me do something special, something lasting and significant for Him, but He just allowed all those possibilities to be taken away from me. In my mind, God had failed me. He had left me hopeless, alone, embarrassed, and broken. Because of these feelings, I wanted nothing more to do with Him. I was now completely lost because I had dismissed in my heart the One who truly loved me and the only One in this world who could help me.

Looking back at this time of my life, I realize I was very immature spiritually and, as a result, I responded very poorly to this challenge. Thankfully, even though I left and ignored Him, God never left or gave up on me. He immediately provided me with an opportunity, a distraction, a bridge to help ease some of my deep pain and anguish.

CHAPTER 11

SHOW BIZ?

The year was 1989. George H.W. Bush became the forty-first president of the United States. A 6.9 magnitude earthquake hit the San Francisco Bay area, killing sixty-three people. The supertanker Exxon Valdez ran aground in Prince William Sound, Alaska, spilling over ten million gallons of oil into the ocean and causing extensive environmental damage. The dividing wall in Berlin, Germany, came down. And in Beijing, China, more than 2,700 demonstrators were massacred in Tiananmen Square.

Also in 1989, the average individual income was $20,220 a year, the median cost of a new house was $120,000, the average cost to rent an apartment was $425 a month, and a gallon of gas was a dollar. The top movies playing in the theaters were "Batman," "Field of Dreams," "Rain Man," "When Harry Met Sally," "Glory," and "Do the Right Thing." The top music hits were "Love Shack" by the B-52s, "My Prerogative" by Bobby Brown, "Girl You Know It's True" by Milli

Vanilli, "Bust A Move" by Young MC, "Straight Up" by Paula Abdul, and "Funky Cold Medina" by Tone Loc.

It was about this time that I received a phone call from a woman I had worked with five years earlier, as a customer service agent for FedEx at their western regional call center. She asked if I would model in a fashion show the company was putting on at the Red Lion Inn to raise money for the homeless in the Sacramento area. Even though I had never modeled before, I said yes. I had lots of fun, and the show was a big success.

A woman approached me afterwards and said I did a great job. She asked me what modeling school taught me how to work the ramp the way I did. I thanked her for the compliment but told her I never went to any school, I was just playing around and having fun doing what I had seen models do on TV. She asked if I'd be interested in modeling again, and I said no. I told her I hadn't modeled before, and I that only modeled that night for FedEx to help the cause of the homeless. She then said she managed a modeling troupe and was willing to pay me two hundred dollars a show to model. To prance across a runway a few times? That sounded like easy money to me, so I said I'd give it a try.

A month later I was in my first real fashion show. This modeling thing was fun, and it was a quick and easy way to make some extra money. After modeling in a few more shows, I invited my siblings to come and watch. Afterwards, my sisters told me I was very good and that I should go to one of the local talent agencies to see what they thought.

I went to a talent agency called Manikin Manor to be evaluated. They liked what they called my "look" and loved the way I walked, but they said that at five feet ten inches tall, I would not make it as a fashion runway model. They instead suggested I pursue print modeling and acting and asked if they could take a few pictures of me at no charge, to which I said yes.

About a month later, Manikin Manor called to let me know they had submitted their photos of me to someone in Hollywood and they wanted to hire me for a job. *You've got to be kidding,* I thought. *Really? Just from a picture?* They then told me that Cosgrove Meurer Productions, the company that produced the TV show "Unsolved Mysteries," was coming to Sacramento to shoot an episode centered around Folsom Prison, and they wanted to hire me as an actor for one week.

I learned a lot about filming scenes from that experience, and it was a lot of fun just being a part of the production. The work was easy, and the money was great.

Soon after that job, Manikin Manor called me to shoot several print ads, a Folsom Lake Toyota commercial, and a "Sacramento Reads" public service announcement. I was starting to work like crazy in a new career I had never imagined I'd be in.

About two weeks later, I received another call from Manikin Manor saying I was chosen to be in a scene with the great Al Pacino, in a movie called "Frankie and Johnny," directed by Garry Marshall. Garry

Marshall was a blast to work with. He made every minute on the set enjoyable. I could tell he really loved what he was doing.

Since this acting career seemed to be taking off, I decided to take a beginner's acting class during the evenings at Sacramento City College to learn more about the craft. On the first night of class, the instructor asked us to introduce ourselves and talk about ourselves for two minutes. I guess I did alright because after the class, the teacher let me know she was casting and directing a play for the fall semester and asked if I would audition that evening. The play was "To Kill a Mockingbird" by Harper Lee. Since I wasn't familiar with the book or story, she gave me a brief rundown and told me I'd be reading for the part of Tom Robinson. I auditioned, read the script, and was cast that night as Tom Robinson.

The play was supposed to run for six weeks, but because we got glowing reviews from the Sacramento theater community, it was extended to eight weeks. I really enjoyed acting and modeling, it seemed almost too good to be true. It was so easy and happening so fast that I decided I should pray to God about whether this new career was His will for me. This is what I prayed:

God, You know I'm liking this acting and modeling thing because it's fun, it's easy, and the money is great. I don't understand what's going on. I don't know what You're doing or what this is all about. I really appreciate it, but I really didn't need it and if You made it all go away, I'd be okay.

The very next morning, my agent called to say that Universal Studios was coming to Sacramento to film a movie, and I had been selected to be a part of it. When I arrived on set, I had barely been there ten minutes when the producer and lead actor, Edward James Olmos, approached me and chose me for a speaking part in his movie, called "American Me." This role enabled me to get my Screen Actors Guild card and be paid at a much higher rate.

For the next two years after filming "American Me," I signed with several new agencies from Reno to San Francisco and was busy doing commercials, plays, movies, music videos, print ads, and public service announcements.

At this point, it seemed like everyone I knew in the acting and modeling business was telling me I should move to Los Angeles, that the time was right for me to further my career as an actor. In the midst of this, I received a call from the casting director of the highly popular soap opera, "Days of Our Lives," who had received one of my headshots. She asked if I was in L.A., to which I answered no, and then she asked if I had plans to come soon and I told her yes, that I was planning to come that next year. "Be sure you call me before you come," she said. "I'll have work for you."

In the summer of 1993, I began in earnest to work toward getting to L.A. My plans were to transfer my FedEx freight job to Los Angeles International Airport (LAX) but only work part-time and on the night shift so that I could pursue my acting career during the day.

But before I made it to Los Angeles, two things happened that affected how I arrived. First, on Monday, January 17, 1994, the 6.7 magnitude Northridge earthquake hit in the city's San Fernando Valley. It damaged much of the homes, property, and streets in the Valley and surrounding areas. The quake and numerous aftershocks caused great fear, and thousands of San Fernando Valley residents moved away.

Then, on Monday, April 4th, the day after Easter, I learned that my father was dying from AIDS. I was about to end my shift at work when my brother Don sent me an emergency page. I rushed to the bank of phones provided for FedEx drivers in the warehouse and called him. My dad had said he was coming to Sacramento this Easter to worship with us, but he never showed up. Don called him to find out why. When he couldn't reach him, he called his pastor, Pastor Marilyn Gazowsky at The Voice of Pentecost Church in San Francisco, to find out if she knew what may have happened. During the conversation, she asked Don if our father had disclosed to us the challenge he was dealing with. When Don said no, she let him know that our dad had full blown AIDS and was preparing to die.

We drove to our father's home in Oakland and found him sitting alone in the middle of his living room, on his Hammond B3 organ, in a bathrobe, waiting to die. I didn't know what to do. Here is my Daddy, sitting in front of me with a death sentence on him, and all I could do was hug him. I was afraid to hug him because at that time, not much was known about AIDS and HIV and everyone was saying not to touch infected people for fear of getting it. But this was my Daddy. I had lived most of my life without him and wanted to know him and have a relationship with him, and now he was dying.

A few years earlier, my father had left the gay life, repented, and renewed his faith and commitment to God, but now it was me living in total rebellion against God. I didn't want to hear about God, talk about God, or talk to God. I was angry at God.

To provide loving care for our father, my siblings and I decided we would bring him home to Sacramento and care for him. We each pledged to take turns caring for him one month at a time. There were six of us, and we all had nice homes, so we felt that was the easiest way we could give Daddy great love and care without any of us burning out.

My sister Shaunielle and her husband Sam volunteered to care for Daddy first. After I finished work each evening, I would hurry home, clean up, and hustle over to their house to spend time with him.

During our time together, we talked and tried to catch up on the many years we had been apart. I asked him to play the piano, which brought back memories of having my dad around when I was a young child, sitting next to him in church while he played the piano or organ. Many times during these visits, he asked me to read the Bible to him, mostly from the book of Psalms. It was killing me, tearing me up inside, because I really didn't want to read the Bible or hear anything about God.

But because I loved my dad and my dad loved God, that's where most of the conversations would end up. My father knew I wasn't really walking with God, and I knew that he knew, but he was a very kind and gracious man. He never said a word to me about my commitment to God. He just subtly kept asking me to read the Word to him and as I did, every time, God's Word pounded on my heart's door big time.

As the days progressed, Daddy's body got weaker and weaker. He lasted maybe a month in all. In a matter of mere days, he went from walking tall, talking strong, and playing the piano, to riding in a wheelchair, asking to nap after two-minute conversations, and needing to be on constant oxygen. Each day our dad was slowly running out of energy, life's energy, the basic energy to walk, talk, and breathe. At a certain point, his breathing got so bad, we had to admit him to the hospital.

I vividly remember my father's last two nights at the Kaiser Hospital South Sacramento. He, my brother Don, and I had several deep conversations about life. I knew he was getting close to death, and I wanted to find out as much as I could about him and the life he had lived all those years after he left. Daddy was on his deathbed, in his final hours, and I wanted to know the truth—the good, the bad, the ugly, all of it!

So, I asked my father, where did he go? Where had he been all these years? He said he had been all over. He had been around the world several times with friends and associates in the gay community. When I asked him what they were doing, he said they were most of the time planning and discussing the gay movement and how to make that lifestyle normal and accepted. He told me there were thousands of gay men and women in every sector of life, the educational system, the entertainment industry, the government system, the sports arena, the legal system, and the political arena just waiting to do what he called "coming out of the closet."

I asked Daddy about the gay life. How did he get there? What was the allure of that lifestyle? What kept him in it so long? And why or how did he come out of it? He said it was a need and hunger for affirmation, and in the gay world, everyone is affirmed. "Have you ever noticed how gays greet each other?", he asked me. "They don't just greet each other, they celebrate each other." He explained that when you've never been affirmed or celebrated by anyone, especially if you've always felt like an outcast or misfit, once you begin to receive that kind of affirmation and attention, it's like a drug you just can't get enough of because you've been without it so long.

Daddy further explained that everyone thinks the gay lifestyle is all about the sex, parties, and living wildly, but he said it was always about affirmation. That's what captivated him about the gay lifestyle, and that's why he stayed in it so long. Living life affirmed for him was addictive! He told us that, in almost every case, male or female, there is a lack of affirmation from the father, a father figure, or the dominant male role model in the family. He added that if the church could learn how to love and express love like gays do, there would be long lines of people in front of every church in America.

Something else my father shared is that gays are going to tell everyone they were born that way. But he vehemently refuted that concept as just the argument they use to help make their lifestyle acceptable and legitimate. Rather, he said, it was a spiritual thing just like everything else, and that one must not give into the temptations and enticements of this spirit. I was amazed by how candidly and completely my father answered each question about his life in the gay world. He was dying and he knew it, and he didn't hold anything back.

The next night, Saturday, May 7, 1994, my dad gave instructions to Don and me about his final arrangements. He told us where all his important final papers were, where his burial plot was, what kind of gravestone he wanted, and what he wanted it to say. He told us what color coffin he had selected and who would direct his funeral. He told us what clothes he wanted his body to be dressed in.

Daddy then asked what kind of items each one of us siblings needed, because several of his friends had preceded him in death and left many of their possessions to him. I cried and told him I didn't want any of his things, I just wanted him to fight and live. I was in total denial, telling him and the doctors he wasn't going to die. Even in my state of anger and rebellion against God, I was still hoping and praying that God would miraculously heal my father and give me the time I so badly wanted with him. Little did I know that the doctors had already started the morphine drip.

When it was time to go home that evening, we hugged and kissed our Daddy good night. I remember the conversation so well, because it would be our last. He looked at me with a smile on his face.

"Son, live for God," he gently urged me.

"Yes, Daddy," I replied, "I'll live for God; I promise you." I then said, "Good night, Daddy. I'll see you in the morning."

"Yes, son, I'll see you in the morning."

We all left the hospital and went to our respective homes, thinking we'd see him the next day. But an hour later, we got the call from the hospital, informing us our Daddy had passed. We all rushed back to the hospital to be with him. All six of us joined hands in a circle around his body and gave thanks to God for his life, his salvation, and the time we had with him.

It was at that moment, seeing my father dead, the one whom I came from, that the reality of my own mortality came into full view. I had been around death before. Someone had even died in my arms once, a stabbing victim when I was nineteen years old. but I could never imagine myself dying. That night, it became crystal clear to me that I would someday have to face my own death.

After we prayed and sent our sisters off, Don, our little brother Stephan, and I, said goodbye one last time to our Daddy. We placed him in the body bag, zipped it up, and left the hospital.

Even though I was not actively walking with God, I ended up delivering the eulogy for my dad's homegoing service because I wanted it to be a true celebration of his life. I didn't want to give anyone the chance to mess up the testimony and blessing of what God had done in my father's life.

On Saturday, June 4, 1994, I made another life-changing decision and moved to L.A. I packed up all my belongings into a U-Haul truck and moved to sunny Southern California—Van Nuys in the San Fernando Valley, to be exact— to further pursue my acting career. On my very first day there, I went into a Ralph's grocery store to shop with my children Brandon and Dani, and who do we run into but Forest Whitaker. Our first Hollywood celebrity!

This was a very exciting time for me. I soon saw many well- known people every day. Paula Abdul and Lela Rochon at Starbucks in the mornings, Wilt Chamberlain and Natalie Cole at the gym, Richard Dreyfuss at the Baskin Robbins 31 Flavors, Al Jarreau and Liam Neeson at the post office. It was like I was in some wonderful but weird dream because, for majority of my life, I had focused on music or sports. So, what was I doing here? How did I get here in Los Angeles as an actor? I never planned to be or wanted to be an actor.

During the next few years, I had the opportunity to meet many new people and have many new experiences. I worked on movies, television, plays, commercials, and print ads with many of the world's most well-known and talented people. They included Eddie Murphy, John Travolta, Will Smith, Laura Linney, Dick Clark, Charlie Sheen, Robert Townsend, Ellen Degeneres, Martin Lawrence, Tim Curry, Ernie

Hudson, John Hawkes, and Martin Sheen. It was wonderful! It was exciting and the money was awesome!

But deep inside, I was still restless and somewhat frustrated. Restless, because I didn't have inner peace because I missed my close relationship with God. Frustrated, because at that time, Hollywood wasn't telling the kinds of stories I wanted to be a part of, or at least I wasn't getting the opportunities to be in the kinds of movies I preferred. I wanted to be in stories that educated the world about the significant, historical contributions African Americans had made to society. Instead, I was getting offers to play pimps, Mack Daddies, drug dealers, drug addicts, or gang members. I was even offered to be a Chippendale's dancer. But I didn't want to play any role that further perpetuated the negative stereotypes so many people already associated with African Americans. More importantly, I did not want my children to see me doing anything that might show me in a negative light.

Still, my acting career was going well and I was working so steadily that I was able to quit my job with FedEx. It was a bittersweet landmark of time in my life. Bitter, because after fourteen years of service, I was leaving a great job with a great company, but sweet, because I could finally be totally focused on whatever I wanted to. That was something to celebrate. So, the morning after my last night of work at FedEx, I took all my company gear—hats, coats, shirts, sweaters, shorts, and slacks—to the dumpster and had my own private FedEx retirement celebration. I thanked God for leading me to FedEx and all the years

He allowed me to work there, but I also thanked Him for the new opportunities I now had. I also thanked Him for helping me and caring for me when I was about to go off the rails, because for a minute there, I was really in an unsound state of mind.

CHAPTER 12

THE KINGDOM

Sometime around 1996, things inside of me began to change. I enjoyed the Hollywood scene with all its excitement, people, and work, but I just wasn't satisfied. They still weren't telling the kinds of stories I wanted to tell, and I was unfulfilled. I felt empty because something was missing. I guess most people would have been super excited to be in the midst of the Hollywood scene, but I wasn't.

In late 1996 or early 1997 I started attending a church in Studio City, California, called In His Presence Church, pastored by Mel and Desiree Ayres. Soon, I began to give into the loving and gentle nudges of the Holy Spirit tugging at my heart strings. I could hear God asking me to come home, telling me He loved me, and inviting me to start our relationship afresh.

The Lord made me aware that He had never left me and never would. He told me He would heal me, help me, be with me, and show me Himself in ways I had never seen before. It wasn't long before I made the decision to recommit my life to Him. My girlfriend followed my lead, and within a year we were married. After a year or so, on October 22, 1998, we were blessed with a beautiful and very gifted baby girl we named Gabrielle Lorene Monique.

During this time, I developed a voracious appetite for the Word of God. My prayer and fasting life went through the roof. I really began to pursue God in any and every way I could. I just wanted more and more of Him. I began attending Bible classes, seminars, workshops, conferences, and anything I thought would strengthen, motivate, and encourage me in the things of God. As a result, I began to have many dreams and see visions inspired by the Holy Spirit.

THE BURNING BUSH

It was now 1999. President Bill Clinton was being impeached. Two students at Columbine High School in Colorado killed thirteen people in an unprecedented mass shooting, shocking the nation. Also, Tiger Woods won his first PGA championship. The average individual income was $36,476 a year, the median cost of a new home was $161,000, the average cost to rent an apartment was $646 a month, and the cost of gas was one dollar and sixty-two cents a gallon.

The top movies playing in the theaters in 1999 were 'Star Wars: The Phantom Menace," "The Green Mile," "American Pie," "The Mummy," and "The Matrix." "SpongeBob Square Pants," "Beverly Hills 90210," "Frazier," and "Sex in the City" were the big hits on television. And on the music scene, Ricky Martin was "Livin' La Vida Loca," Britney

Spears was singing "Baby One More Time," TLC was complaining about "No Scrubs," and Eminem was spittin' "The Real Slim Shady."

But as for me, early in the spring of 1999, I felt a prompting of the Holy Spirit to move to Valencia, California, and start a church. I initially argued with God, reasoning that African Americans made up only about two percent of the total population in this suburb in the Santa Clarita Valley, about forty-one miles north-north-west Downtown Los Angeles. But God immediately settled that issue with this question: "What does My Word say in John 3:16?"

Well, John 3:16 says, "For God so loved *the world* that he gave his only begotten Son, that whosoever believeth in him should not perish, but have everlasting life" (KJV, emphasis added). The Holy Spirit reminded me that Jesus came to save the world, not black men, and not white men, but all men. He made it very clear to me that He was not sending me to Valencia to preach the gospel to African Americans and that I was never again to think about people in terms of color or race. God was sending me to Valencia to share the story of His everlasting and unconditional love for *all* people.

I then began to argue that whites would never accept the gospel from me, a black man from Northern California. God then brought to my attention that my excuses were just like the excuses Moses gave Him when He told him to go free the Israelites from Pharaoh in Egypt. He reminded me of what He did for and through Moses. He let me know again that I was to go and share the good news of His saving grace with everyone. God let me know that what He had given me, the

147

city of Valencia needed. He told me not to worry but to go boldly in faith and leave the details to Him.

God then instructed me to name the church The Burning Bush Church. We visited Valencia several times to look for a place to live and a place to start the church, but we couldn't find either one. Still, we continued to think and plan as if we would. Finally, after much prayer, I decided to approach the Hyatt Valencia Hotel with the intention of starting the church there.

At the time, the Hyatt Valencia was a brand new, higher-end hotel in downtown Valencia, and it was having trouble filling its rooms. I didn't know that to be fact, but I suspected it. If we could have church services there, it would give people in the area another reason to come. They could see the new hotel and the new church in town in one visit, creating a win-win situation for both The Burning Bush Church and the Hyatt Valencia.

When I went to inquire about renting space at the Hyatt Valencia, I was introduced to the manager of banquet room reservations. I introduced myself, told her my desire to use one of their rooms to start a church, and shared my vision of us working together in a win-win situation. I told her I felt God had called me to Valencia to make a positive spiritual impact in the city and that the church would be a blessing to the community.

When I let her know what I could afford to pay each month for use of the rooms on Sundays, we were about a thousand dollars apart from coming to an agreement. I knew I didn't have any more money but I really wanted to secure this place for the church. When I started explaining to her that I was a covenant man, she stopped me at that point and told me she was Jewish and understood what covenant meant. I then said that, if she would work with me to allow our church to gather there, God would bless her. I asked if she had a specific need that I could pray for, and she suddenly began to cry, telling me that she and her husband had been trying to conceive for several years with no success. I offered to pray with her about her heart's desire, and she said yes. Right then and there, we prayed to the God of Abraham, Isaac, and Jacob and asked that He would bless her with a baby, because she had been a blessing to us.

She arranged for us to have the rooms we wanted at the lower price, and two months later when I went into her office to pay the rent, she came out running towards me with tears of joy in her eyes. "Pastor Les! Pastor Les! I'm pregnant! We are pregnant!" We filled her office that day with joy, praises, and giving glory to God. It was so wonderful to witness the hand of God moving on our behalf. I knew beyond a shadow of doubt that He was with us.

On Sunday, June 6, 1999, we started The Burning Bush Church in the Hyatt Valencia Hotel with seventy-five guests, friends, and well-wishers. After that first Sunday worship service, we were able to start the ministry with about thirty-five regular attendees.

Because of what I could see financially, my plan was to offer services on Sundays only until we could find a more permanent and affordable spot to have a mid-week service or Bible study. But immediately after that first service, a gentleman approached me and asked why we weren't having a mid-week service and why we didn't have a place for the children to meet. I shared with him our financial challenge as a brand-new ministry, and he said don't worry about it.

"We need a mid-week service," he said. "I have grandchildren that I want to know Jesus. Here's my phone number. Call me and let me know what you need to make it happen and I'll have it for you next Sunday."

Isn't that just like God to show up and show off in ways unimaginable? That's just what He did. Because of God's miraculous provision through this generous man, we were able to provide ministry for the children and have a mid-week Bible study for the adults.

That was not the only God-thing that happened that first day. After checking my messages, I was informed that a townhouse three blocks away from the Hyatt Valencia had become available, and my family and I could move in that week.

I also met that day a lady named Dawn Brayton and her son Austin. Dawn would become the first new partner at The Burning Bush Church. That week, she gave birth to another boy named Colton. God would make us family. Her sons became my sons, and we shared together the challenges, joys, and seasons that life brought, and to this day, she and her family continue to be a blessing in my life. Because of what God was doing in Valencia, I was more confident that I had heard Him correctly and that He had called us to the right place at the right time.

We continued to meet for services at the Hyatt for the next six months. Soon, we were able to secure a small store-front facility located at 28030 Copperhill Road, near the corner of Seco Canyon and Copperhill. It had been the former home of the North Park Community Church, which had grown tremendously and needed to move to a larger facility. One of their members informed one of our partners that they were moving, and we were able to strike a deal with the management company before the building hit the market. Wow! Another unexplainable God-thing!

We moved into the Seco Canyon location with great joy and anticipation, but not without some serious challenges along the way. There were several bomb threats and racial slurs directed at the church, and our windows were broken out. The enemy was mad because we were making a positive impact for Christ in the city of Valencia. We remained undaunted. Because this building only seated about 110 people, we leased two other buildings on the same corner, one for our youth ministry and the other for our thriving children's ministry, which met at the La Petite Children's Academy across the street.

We continued worshipping at this location for three years. Here, God blessed us with a young, vibrant, truly multicultural church of about 135 partners, many of them with significant leadership ability. Our church was fueled by and heavily dependent on prayer. Because so many of our partners worked in the city of Los Angeles, our main weekly prayer service was on Tuesday mornings from 5:00 to 6:00 a.m.

On Tuesday, September 11, 2001, as I was about to leave after our regular prayer meeting, a flood of phone calls came in from church partners asking if I knew what was going on. They told me that an American Airlines jet crashed into one of the Twin Towers in New York City. I only lived five minutes away from the church, so I hurried home and arrived just in time to see the second plane make impact.

The horrific events of that day affected and changed everything and everyone in the United States of America. As things unfolded, it became apparent that the United States of America had been attacked by enemy forces on our own soil, in New York City, one of the most densely populated cities in the world.

Who would do such a thing? Who would be so bold and audacious as to attack the United States of America, one of the most powerful countries in the world? Who was responsible for this heinous act, and where were they? The United States of America would now be ushered into a whole new era of fear, vulnerability, and uncertainty. Americans were nervous, afraid, angry, and looking for answers. Across the nation, Americans were worried and wondering if our country would ever be safe again. The events of 9/11 brought United States citizens together and ignited the spirit of patriotism through the roof.

As a result of this new season of fear and uncertainty, our church quickly grew to about 170 partners. We were already having three worship services on Sundays, so we began looking for a larger facility. Soon we located, secured, and moved into a 6,000 square foot building in a strip mall located at 27737 Bouquet Canyon Road.

In the next few years, The Burning Bush Church exploded to just over 500 partners. I was now leading a vibrant, hungry, vision-driven church, full of active and excited partners who allowed us to offer many different types of ministries to our community. These ministries included a children's ministry, a youth ministry, Bible class, marriage counseling, business and leadership forums and seminars, Vacation Bible School, a praise and worship team, a gospel choir, and a weekly, half-hour cable TV program called "The Burning Bush Experience."

In addition, our church actively provided physical and financial support to the Santa Clarita Crisis Pregnancy Center, the Santa Clarita Senior Center, the Fellowship of Christian Athletes, Alcoholic Anonymous, Campus Crusade for Christ Ministries founder Bill Bright and his Jesus Film Project, Bishop T. D. Jakes and The Potter's House (TPH) International Pastoral Alliance, and many more organizations and ministries.

Our vision was to be a ministry that:
1. was committed to fasting and prayer for divine direction;

2. would forever evangelize the lost;

3. would teach people how to enter into a personal and intimate relationship with God;

4. would build and advance the Kingdom of God through financial empowerment and the mass media;

5. would produce change and growth as a result of teaching biblical principles;

6. promoted unity in the body of Christ with no racial barriers;

7. was involved in the community;

8. by faith would build mortgage-free facilities to house community programs;

9. was committed to providing love, guidance, and support to all people regardless of race, creed, or position in life;

10. was committed to making a lasting impact on the Santa Clarita Valley, the state of California, the United States of America, and the world by training, empowering, and sending ministers into the worldwide harvest of souls.

It was so wonderful to watch God work and to be a part of what He was doing. He seemed to bless everything that was going on at The Burning Bush Church. We were on fire and excited about taking new ground for the Kingdom. Souls were being saved, lives were being changed, and God was being glorified.

And then, out of nowhere, amid all this great momentum, we got a letter from the City of Santa Clarita requesting to meet with The Burning Bush Church, our lawyers, our landlord, and his lawyers concerning the building we were leasing. During our time at this location the city had annexed the area where the church was located, and this changed the status of our conditional use permit.

All the parties met at Valencia City Hall. It was disclosed that, due to safety regulations, the city wanted us to build a firewall between our main sanctuary and a room we used as our church office and youth center. The estimated construction cost was somewhere around $20,000. The landlord and I came to an agreement that the church would finance the firewall, and he and his construction team would handle the installation.

At the conclusion of the meeting, I was very happy because we were staying in this building that had served us so well in positively impacting our community for Christ. But, while we all were walking to our cars, the landlord's attorney called our attorney over and told him the landlord changed his mind and no longer wanted to do what he had agreed to do just minutes ago in the presence of the city lawyers. He then informed us that we had to vacate the building in sixty days!

Really? What can we do? Where can we go? What is this all about? Lord, what is happening? Is this a test? Did we do something wrong? Did we step outside of Your will? How can we save the ministry? These were just a few of the questions swimming around in my head.

After weeks of intense research and inquiry concerning a new worship location in the Santa Clarita area, we shared with the congregation that our best option was to hold services at a local movie theater multiplex in the neighboring suburb of Canyon Country and save our funds until something more conducive became available.

To conduct worship services in Canyon Country meant that many of our partners had to drive a little further than before and that all of us had to pitch in with moving, setting up, and tearing down several rooms of furniture, sound equipment, and musical instruments every week. It was hard and tedious work and many in the congregation did not embrace it. Only seventy partners showed up that first Sunday at the theater for worship services. We were missing more than 300-plus partners.

My wife and I were shocked, hurt, and disappointed. How could the people that we had loved and faithfully served just get up and go, and with no good-bye or explanation? They were just gone. Where did they go? I honestly don't know where, but looking back in retrospect, I really can't blame them. It was like a bad dream. You're a part of this wonderful, thriving ministry with everything in place and suddenly— boom! —you're starting all over again with no permanent place to meet. The reality of the situation was stunning, and it hurt.

This sudden, difficult, and hurtful situation had a tremendous negative effect on my wife, as she began to experience a level of stress that caused her to suffer several back-to-back illnesses, diverticulitis, and fibromyalgia, to name a few. We tried to continue the ministry for a few more years and even moved to several smaller locations trying to be financially responsible. But, in the end, we had to shut the ministry down.

FCA

I was hurt, confused, and devoid of a plan or solution. I felt like my purpose had been snatched right out from under my feet. I really needed to hear from God concerning His will for my life, not only for my sake but for the sake of my wife and family. So, I intensified my efforts to hear from Him. I began to pray even more earnestly and one morning decided I would not leave my bedroom until God made it clear to me about what He wanted me to do.

I laid on that floor for at least three to four hours crying out to God for answers. I waited there until I finally heard Him speak. In a calm and gentle voice, "F-C-A."

FCA? I thought. Well, I knew about FCA because as a teenager more than thirty-five years ago, I gave my life to Christ at an FCA football camp in Ashland, Oregon. I got up from prayer, went directly to my computer, and googled "FCA," which led me to FCA.org, the website for the Fellowship of Christian Athletes. There I found the name Mark Wracher, a Los Angeles County representative. There was no phone number for Mark, only an email address, so I sent him the following message:

Hello, my name is Les Robinson. I am the founder and senior pastor of The Burning Bush Church in Santa Clarita.

I gave my life to Christ many years ago, when I was in high school at an FCA camp in Ashland, Oregon. How can I help?

About thirty minutes later, Mark called me, introduced himself, and asked if we could meet over a cup of coffee. Later that day, we met at a nearby Starbucks, and I shared with him my FCA story. I told him how I was selected by my football coach to attend FCA camp in Ashland Oregon more than thirty-plus years ago, thinking I was going to a football camp to become better football player but leaving a better person and athlete as a result of what happened to me, what I did there, and who I met there. Namely, Jesus.

Mark said he had never met a person who had made a decision for Christ at FCA camp in their youth and later returned to give their life testimony. He told me that FCA Southern California, which had about 150 workers and volunteers, was getting ready to put on an FCA Sports Camp at University of California, Santa Barbara (UCSB) and my story would inspire his team of coaches and volunteers to press on. Mark later scheduled a pre-camp meeting with his team at UCSB and allowed me to tell them the story of my FCA camp experience. When I finished, there were only a few dry eyes in the place.

While riding home from that pre-camp meeting, Mark said he wanted to hire me but that he couldn't because the economy had just experienced a downturn and he didn't have the funds. I told him I did not call him for a job but that I was now on assignment by God to serve through FCA. I told him I was an assistant football coach at Saugus

High School and would start, run, and finance an FCA Huddle there and work to bring kids to next year's FCA Sports Camp.

Over the next three years, through the FCA Huddles, I helped spread the gospel on several high school campuses in the Santa Clarita Valley. We started them at Saugus High, then Canyon High, followed by Hart High. After three and a half years of serving these schools and sending many young athletes to camp, the new Los Angeles area director, Josh Canales, asked me to join the FCA Southern California staff by faith and trust that God would supply the needed funding. I accepted his invitation. I purposed in my heart to trust God for the funding and support, and He continued to advance the ministry.

Some of the early, founding volunteers were Steve Dixon (who was our first Tom Landry donor, giving $10,000 or more annually), Dustin LaChance, John Hineman, Elaine Hineman, Pastor Bob Bae, and Pastor Ricky Stoner. They all helped open new FCA Huddles at West Ranch High School, Golden Valley High School, Santa Clarita Christian School, Legacy Christian Academy, Valencia High School, Castaic High School, and College of the Canyons. As a result of what God was doing on these campuses through FCA, from 2005 to 2022, nearly 9,000 students made decisions for Christ.

Looking back on how God orchestrated my life, I doubt very seriously I would have witnessed that many decisions for Christ from our church building. I see how God wanted me working outside the four walls of a church. He wanted me to be out on the high seas of life, fishing for men, women, boys, and girls right where they lived. He sent me to the schools, football fields, training facilities, basketball courts, soccer fields, tracks, and baseball and softball fields to win coaches and athletes and those they influence to Christ. What a plan!

But tracking after God didn't come without a price. It came at a great cost. Even though He positioned me to make significant positive impact in the Santa Clarita Valley and used me to influence people toward Him, the devil was not just sitting back and watching us take ground for the Kingdom. The enemy of God and His people was doing his level best to distract, hinder, and discourage us from doing the Lord's will. A few years later, I began to experience the challenges I described in Chapter 1.

CHAPTER 13

LIVING THE LEGACY

Since my discovery of Daniel Blue, the process of my thinking has been challenged, expanded, and transformed. I have a new and greater awareness of who I am and what I am, and of why I am and what I was born to do. I am blessed, honored, and thrilled to be the great-great-great-grandson of Daniel Blue, a very intentional and courageous former enslaved man whom God used to influence and change the trajectory of California, our nation, and the world.

For most of my life, I had been searching for significance, purpose, and legacy. The fact is that, even had I not discovered Daniel Blue, God had already called and chosen me to lead a life of significance, purpose, and legacy with even greater implications than those I share with Daniel Blue, and these implications have eternal value. I had already been called and chosen to be His son, and I was given the ministry of reconciliation, bringing men back to God by teaching and modeling His great, unconditional, and everlasting love.

Daniel Blue was a man used by God to share and distribute His love to his neighbors regardless of creed, color, or station in life. Daniel Blue lived and operated from a position of love, *agape* love, God's love. His selfless life and testimony have challenged me to live a more intentional life, dedicated to loving and helping others.

Jeremiah 29:11 comes to mind: "'For I know the plans I have for you,' declares the LORD. 'They are plans for good and not for disaster, to give you a future and a hope'" (NLT). So, what will I do with this newfound knowledge of where I came from and who I am? I have decided to do all that I can with the time I have left, to move the needle a little further toward human harmony and to continue living the legacy of love that God demonstrated in Daniel Blue.

As Genesis 1:26-27 informs us, we were all created in the image and likeness of God; meaning that we were created to look, think, and operate like Him. And one way to do that is to remember what 1 John 4:7-8 says about the nature and character of God, that love is of God and that God is love. So, I've chosen to take the same path that my great-great-great-grandfather Daniel Blue chose. I've chosen to be like my Heavenly Father and love. I have decided to live a life dedicated to showing and sharing love. I want to love, to teach love, and to be love.

My first commitment is to love God with all my heart, mind, and soul; and then I'm committed to love my fellow man. Even those who don't look like me, think like me, talk like me, pray like me, vote like me, or love like me.

Why? Because nothing is more powerful than love. There is no substitute for it and no defense against it. What the world needs right now is love. We all need it. We can't possibly live without it. The real and complete answer to all our problems—past, present, and future— can be found in love. And, God is love.

1John 4:7-8 (NLT) says,

> "Dear friends, let us continue to love one another, for love comes from God. Anyone who loves is a child of God and knows God. But anyone who does not love does not know God, for God is love."

This passage from God's precious Word reminds me that it was truly in Jesus Christ that I discovered my significance, purpose, and legacy. And it's the legacy of God's love to me, in me, and through me.

You, too, may have an ancestor you're not aware of. My hope and prayer is that, if you do, you will find them. Even more importantly, I pray you discover your rightful place and position with God our Father, because that is when you will discover the unique person God has created and shaped you to be. You are His son, His daughter, His child, created in His image and likeness, innately gifted with the wonderful ability to receive and give love.

I have decided to stick with love. Hate is too great a burden to bear.

—Dr. Martin Luther King Jr.

ACKNOWLEDGMENTS

This book exists only because of a wonderful group of people I call "Team Daniel Blue." They challenged me to write and keep writing. They supported and encouraged me to keep moving forward even though I didn't know where I was going. They helped me with research and found tons of documents and articles. Most of all, they loved and supported me in prayer. Thank you, "Team Daniel Blue." You've been a blessing.

I will always be indebted to you.

Dr. Phillip Allen

Shaunielle Belcher

Susan Christopher

Shevonne Davenport

Cyndi Galley

DISCOVERING DANIEL BLUE

Duane Hodges

Cal Linam

Uumoiya Strother Glass

Willa Robinson & the KP Publishing Team

Robin Rositani

Yvonne Westover Robinson

Jeannie Anderson-West

ABOUT THE AUTHOR

Pastor Les Robinson is a true Bible scholar and teacher whose messages, for over forty years, have inspired, challenged, and encouraged believers and non-believers alike to surrender their lives to God and pursue a real and life-changing relationship with Jesus Christ.

Surviving the dangerous and drug-infested streets of Sacramento, California's "Oak Park," on the way to becoming an athlete, coach, musician, actor, and pastor provided a complex yet abundant wealth of experiences and wisdom upon which he draws.

In 1999, Pastor Les Robinson founded the Burning Bush Church in Santa Clarita, California, where he served as Senior Pastor for fourteen years.

In 2006, he began serving as the Director of Ministry for the Fellowship of Christian Athletes in the Santa Clarita Valley. He started eleven campus huddles and witnessed over 8,639 young people make decisions for Christ.

He has served as an interim pastor for the International Foursquare Gospel Ministries in Mojave, California, and is currently the Men's Ministry Pastor at The Sanctuary Foursquare Church in Santa Clarita, California.

Pastor Les Robinson is the great-great-great-grandson of Daniel Blue, the California pioneer and former slave who discovered gold, founded the first African American church west of the Mississippi River, and ended slavery in California in 1864.

Pastor Les is married to his lovely wife, Yvonne, and is the father of two sons, three daughters, and four grandchildren. His life goal is to serve God by serving His people and to hear His Master say, "Well done, thou good and faithful servant."

MILESTONES IN THE LIFE AND LEGACY OF DANIEL BLUE

DATE	KEY EVENT
March 1, 1796	Daniel Blue is born in Monroe County, Kentucky.
1824	Lucinda Luny is born in Montgomery County, Alabama.
January 24, 1848	Gold discovered at Sutter's Mill in Coloma, California, by James Marshall. Gold Rush begins.
August 1849	80,000-plus people come to the Sacramento, California, area, calling themselves the "Forty-Niners."

September 2, 1849	At age fifty-three, Daniel Blue arrives in Sacramento on a wagon train with John Dougherty, the younger brother of Daniel's enslaver, Mason Doherty. Daniel Blue discovers gold and buys property at 4th and I Streets; establishes a laundry business.
December 20, 1849	Peter Hardeman Burnett becomes California's first governor.
August 9,1850	Daniel Blue marries Lucinda Luny; they become the second couple to be officially married in Sacramento. Daniel Blue begins Bethel Church (later renamed St. Andrews AME Church) with Barney and George Fletcher in his home, California's first black church and the first AME church west of the Mississippi River.
September 9, 1850	California becomes the thirty-first state of the Union. By this time, over 300,000 people from all over the world have descended on the Sacramento Valley.
January 9, 1851	John McDougal becomes the second governor of California.

1851	Wooden building of St. Andrews AME Church (Bethel) is completed, and its 27-member congregation moves in. Son William Blue is born.
January 8, 1852	John Bigler becomes the third governor of California and will become the first to serve two terms.
1853	Son Daniel Blue Jr. is born.
1854	School for African Americans, Native Americans, Latin Americans, and Asian Americans begins in St. Andrews AME Church's basement.
November 20–22, 1855	St. Andrews AME Church hosts the first State Convention of Colored Citizens of California, focusing on black (male) voter rights.
1855	Daughter Laura Blue is born.
1856	Second State Convention of Colored Citizens held at St. Andrews AME Church, focusing on blacks' right to testify in court against whites.
1857	Daughter Henrietta is born.

1859	The California Gold Rush ends. An estimated total of two billion dollars' worth of gold was extracted, and 3,000-plus slaves were brought to California mainly from Arkansas, Kentucky, Missouri, and Texas.
1860	Home at 9th and F Streets set on fire by arson. Son William dies at age 9 of congested lungs, suspected from smoke inhalation due to the fire.
1861	Daughter Annie Blue is born.
April 12, 1861	American Civil War begins at Fort Sumter, South Carolina.
1863	The Transcontinental Railroad begins construction. Law allowing African American men to vote passes. Law allowing African Americans to testify in court against whites passes. Someone attempts to burn down St. Andrews school.

1864	Daniel Blue secures freedom in court for twelve-year-old slave girl named Edith (Adda) from Walter Gammon, formally ending slavery in California.
December 22, 1864	Laura Blue dies at age 9.
1865	House at 9th and F Streets is taken in a $1,200 lawsuit judgement (case unclear) against Daniel and Lucinda Blue.
May 9, 1865	American Civil War ends after four years and twenty-seven days of fighting, with over 650,000 lives lost and four million slaves freed. St. Andrews AME Church hosts another State Convention of Colored Citizens of California, focusing on the abolishment of segregated schools in California.
1867	Construction begins on a new brick building for St. Andrews AME Church.
1869	The Transcontinental Railroad is completed.
1871	Daniel Blue is appointed as a porter for the California State Assembly. Daniel Blue is named rear porter for the gubernatorial inauguration of Newton Booth.

1873	Daughters Annie and Henrietta Blue are granted permission to attend Sacramento Grammar School, becoming the first African Americans to learn with whites.
1875	Annie Blue graduates from Sacramento Grammar School.
1880	Daniel Blue is selected with other prominent black citizens to meet and greet President Rutherford B. Hayes, the first sitting U.S. president to travel west of the Colorado Rockies.
October 15, 1884	Daniel Blue dies at age 88.
1886	Hazel Johnson White, Daniel's Blue's granddaughter, is born.
August 31, 1899	Lucinda Luny Blue dies at age 75.
September 28, 1908	Lola White Reed, Daniel Blue's great-granddaughter, is born.
March 3, 1934	Lester Robinson Jr. is born.
January 4, 1935	Janet Turner, Les Robinson III's mother, is born.
1951	St. Andrews AME Church relocates to 8th and U Streets.

October 20, 1956	Lester Robinson III is born.
December 17, 1962	Hazel Johnson White, Daniel Blue's granddaughter, dies at age 80.
May 7, 1994	Lester Robinson Jr. dies at age 60.
January 14, 2013	Lola White Reed dies at age 105.
July 15, 2017	Les Robinson discovers Daniel Blue.

BIBLIOGRAPHY

MEDIA CLIPS

Podcast interview with Cyndi Galley on " A New Thing Live"

https://www.youtube.com/watch?v=vWilgJTrwjA&t=1411s

News segment on ABC 10 Sacramento

https://www.abc10.com/amp/article/news/local/daniel-blue-founder
-of-the-first-black-church-pacific-coast/103-3415fccb-c6de-427a
-ace6-378ee9fa6db7

News segment on NBC's "The Today Show"

https://www.youtube.com/watch?v=d9qngGOa1yY

Testimony at California Reparations Task Force Committee hearings
in Oakland, California (beginning at the 1:22:30 mark)

https://youtu.be/zPoVBXJv53M

SOURCE REFERENCES

"Daniel Blue, An African American Pioneer," Rootsweb.com, February 2005.

https://sites.rootsweb.com/~aagriots/CA/DBlue.htm

"How the Founder of California's First Black Church Fought Its Last Known Slavery Case," by Asal Ehsanipour, *The California Report Magazine,* KQED.org, February 25, 2022.

https://www.kqed.org/news/11818409/how-the-founder-of-californias -first-black-church-fought-its-last-known-slavery-case

"Rescue of a Slave Child," *Gold Chains: The Hidden History of Slavery in California,* American Civil Liberties Union (ACLU) of Northern California, ACLUNC.org, May 16, 2020.

https://www.aclunc.org/sites/goldchains/explore/edith-and-daniel -blue.html#:~:text=In%20early%201864%2C%20Blue%2C %20noticed,was%20living%20with%20him%20freely

www.ingramcontent.com/pod-product-compliance
Lightning Source LLC
Chambersburg PA
CBHW051151120626
46547CB00012B/1032